ME AND MR WELLES

TRAVELLING EUROPE WITH A HOLLYWOOD LEGEND

DORIAN BOND

The History Press

For my darling wife, with love and appreciation.

Front Cover: The habitual cigar. (Author's Collection)

First published 2018

The History Press
The Mill, Brimscombe Port
Stroud, Gloucestershire, GL5 2QG
www.thehistorypress.co.uk

© Dorian Bond, 2018

The right of Dorian Bond to be identified as the Author
of this work has been asserted in accordance with the
Copyright, Designs and Patents Act 1988.

British Library Cataloguing in Publication Data.
A catalogue record for this book is available from the British Library.

ISBN 978 0 7509 8586 4

Typesetting and origination by The History Press
Printed in Great Britain

ME AND
MR WELLES

Contents

Introduction

This memoir has been written about events that happened fifty years ago, during the 1960s. The Six-Day War in the Middle East, had just been and gone as I took my final student exams and we were in the midst of what *The New Yorker* has called one of the most tumultuous decades of the twentieth century. So, the reader must forgive inaccuracies on exact dates, but the vast majority of it was taken from my increasingly accurate memory and the copious notes I took at the time in my little hotel room in Rome. It is all true. It is all history, although Orson Welles was dubious about written history, saying it was always written by the winners.

But I was not a winner, or a loser in these events. I was merely a participant – a witness. It was all a remarkable experience with a remarkable man, which I still cherish to this day. To paraphrase Hemingway, if you are lucky enough to have worked for Orson Welles as a young man, then the experience will go with you for the rest of your life, for Orson Welles is a moveable feast.

A feast he was, and I ate my fill.

There are few giants in this world of pygmies and he was one. To quote Shakespeare's Cassius:

He doth bestride the narrow world
Like a Colossus, and we petty men
Walk under his huge legs and peep about
To find ourselves dishonourable graves.

The boy who grew up in Kenosha, Wisconsin, attended the Todd School outside Chicago, turned down a scholarship to Harvard and instead headed out into the world to seek his fame and his fortune, was truly a renaissance man.

His ashes now lie in faraway Andalusia, free from the chaos of his life and the art which gave us all such a unique vision. I was lucky enough to have been up close and personal with him. I salute his memory. As he always said to me, 'Nobody gets justice. People only get good luck or bad luck.'

I lived long enough in China to realise that he was dead right. The Chinese set great store on luck, but what supersedes success or failure is the importance of being true to yourself. Orson Welles never let us down in this respect, so I originally thought of calling this book, *The Importance of Being Orson*.

Whatever it's called doesn't really matter. It's about him.

Dorian Bond
Winchester, England, 2018

'The time has come,' the Walrus said,
'To talk of many things:
Of shoes – and ships – and sealing-wax –
Of cabbages – and kings –
And why the sea is boiling hot –
And whether pigs have wings.'

Lewis Carroll

1

A Dalmatian Meeting

'Dorian St George Bond! With a name like that, you've just gotta be a movie director!' roared Orson Welles. When Orson Welles roared, it could be heard a mile away. Literally.

He was towering over me, which he obviously would do, given that he was a good 6ft something in his socks – I was a flattering 5ft 8in, and anyway, he was standing on the side of a luxury sailing yacht already a couple of feet above the level of the jetty I was standing, or cowering, on.

He was wearing the famous black fedora hat, a black shirt buttoned to the collar, a black suit and black shoes. He was not to wear anything else during the time I was with him. It was a kind of style or uniform that he was comfortable with. It looked good. A Montecristo was sticking out of his mouth, half smoked and half chewed.

All in all, he was a magnificent figure, the image very much reflecting the legend. He might as well have been Charles Foster Kane.

★

'Can you go to Yugoslavia tomorrow for Orson Welles?'

'Yes,' I answered, without missing a beat. They say to be impulsive is a bad thing. This time it was definitely a good thing.

The telephone had just rung and an old lady's voice, very Miss Marple, had asked, 'Is that Dorian Bond?' I had said yes and she had continued, 'My name is Ann Rogers, I'm Orson Welles's private secretary. Can you go to Yugoslavia tomorrow for Mr Welles?'

I confirmed my original reply.

It was the late autumn of 1968: the Battle of Khe Sanh had been fought and lost, and the Tet Offensive had finally been suppressed after savage combat in Huế, immortalised by those dramatic Don McCullin photographs of US Marines fighting and dying in the ruins of the ancient city. In March, I had taken part in the protest against the war in Vietnam which ended with violence in Grosvenor Square. In April, Martin Luther King had been assassinated in Memphis, while in May, Danny Cohn-Bendit had manned the barricades in Paris, and in June, Bobby Kennedy had been assassinated in Los Angeles.

The Prague Spring, which had brought us the sympathetically sad face of Alexander Dubček, had blossomed on his accession to power in January and died with the Eastern Bloc armed forces brutally suppressing the Czechoslovak people at the end of August as the West looked on. Yale had decided to accept women undergraduates, and Richard Nixon had been elected president, completing his comeback from his close-run defeat to Kennedy in 1960 and the humiliation of his failure to win the governorship of California in 1964. Finally, the Troubles in Northern Ireland were just about to begin.

I had sat next to Paul McCartney and Jane Asher and been introduced to Eric Burden, he of 'Rising Sun' fame, at the legendary Scotch in Masons Yard in St James's, that cooler than cool place where Jimi Hendrix had played his first time in London, where the Rolling Stones hung out and where McCartney met Stevie Wonder. I really thought I had my finger on the pulse of contemporary London.

It was a long time ago. Or so it seems to me now.

One evening, I had supper with two friends of mine from university. He had started in the considered world of publishing while she was drifting from job to job. Fiona told me that she had just run an errand for Orson Welles.

'Orson Welles?' I nearly choked on my mouthful of goulash. 'You ran an errand for Orson Welles? Amazing! Did you actually meet him?'

'Yes,' she said airily as if it was the most normal thing in the world to do, run an errand for Orson Welles.

I have to point out to you here that I was at film school, where Orson Welles was not merely a mortal man – he was worshipped as a god by teachers and students alike. There were posters of him in his fedora all around; in fact, those black and white images of him in a number of his films fitted seamlessly on the dank, blackened brick walls of the film school which had once been a fruit and vegetable warehouse. You almost expected him to appear out of the shadows, like Harry Lime, as you mounted the dark stone stairs or turned any corner.

And now, out of the blue sea of the Mediterranean, unbeknownst to him and unbeknownst to me, we seemed to be within touching distance.

And delicious chance had been the instigator, as it is of most things in our lives. Predestination, the Calvinists of Geneva called it. Fate, *fado*, *fatalite*, *sino*, *Schicksal*, or whatever word you want to use.

Human beings, for some reason, are always surprised by change, hostile to change, uncomfortable with change. It's as if we think the rhythm of life will never change. It gives us that feeling of security. When that rhythm does change, we feel insecure, vulnerable, exposed.

But one thing in life is certain: change is inevitable, whether it be a change of pace, a change of location, or a change of personnel. And nobody wants it, expects it, or welcomes it. Most people are afraid of it. But artists create it. By showing us lesser mortals a different way to look at the world, they expose us to this insecurity. It can turn us on, when we hear a particular passage of Shakespeare or a combination of notes by Mozart, or when we look at a juxtaposition of colours by Vincent van Gogh. Or it can disturb us, like a passage from Samuel Beckett or a swathe of orchestral passages from Sibelius or a portrait by Francis Bacon.

Anyway, Fiona had been visiting her tax-exiled parents in Majorca, wondering what to do next with her life. On the beach she had talked to some little children and paddled with them in the clear, azure waters of the Mediterranean. By chance, it transpired they were the grandchildren of an infamous woman. They were the children of the son of none other than the disreputable Lady Docker.

In the dreary 1950s, with England still recovering from postwar rationing and huge swathes of London and many major cities across the land still proudly displaying the burnt-out carcasses of warehouses and industrial buildings bombed by the Luftwaffe, Lady Docker was a byword for poor taste, extravagance and vulgarity all rolled into one. She had illuminated puritanical Britain with enough scandal and ill-chosen remarks to shock every class of person. The upper classes despised her for her vulgar behaviour, while the working classes hated her for her outrageous expenditure in times of such hardship.

Starting out from a modest background in Derbyshire, she moved to London to become a dance hostess, and had married successively three millionaires, rode around in a gold-handled Daimler, spent money like water, and was even banned personally from Monaco by Prince Rainier for tearing up the Monegasque flag on hearing that she could not bring her son Lance to the christening of Prince Albert, to which she and her husband had been invited.

Such is fate. In 1968 she was in Majorca, not the South of France, from which she had also been banned by virtue of an agreement between Monaco and the French Government.

Anyway, her daughter-in-law was sitting on the beach talking to Fiona and was the mother of these children. She lived in sedate Maida Vale, and was a neighbour of a certain Ann Rogers. Maybe she could do something for the floundering Fiona.

On her return to England, Fiona made contact with Mrs Rogers. It transpired that she was the personal secretary of the legendary Orson Welles. So, she was sent on a mission for Orson Welles. She ended up on the Yugoslav coast bearing gifts to Mr Welles of Kodak 35mm raw stock. She stayed a few days and then departed. Unlike me she was not obsessed with movies.

I sat dumbfounded for a few moments, then asked the classic question, 'If Mrs Rogers asks you to do the trip again, can you please give her my name?'

Grant grinned elegantly at me, thinking me mad. He had always reminded me of a Chinese mandarin after a good dinner, or a large Persian cat after it had eaten a mouse. He lived in the urbane world of publishing, where little was done in a hurry and movies were at the bottom of the food chain.

'Of course,' said Fiona.

I thought she was lying – of course she was lying. Who on earth in their right mind would pass up the invitation to go down to the Dalmatian coast and hang out with Orson Welles?

Fortunately, the world is not full of grotty film students.

As I walked home, I put the whole thing out of my mind. Nothing would come of it.

★

'In France all the cineastes became obsessed with my work. I could never understand why! You know, Truffaut and the boring Jean-Luc Godard. He was a Swiss, you know, very rich and always trying to intellectualise film-making. What the hell has existentialism and Marxism got to do with movies? It's a European sickness!'

So true, I thought, as he chuckled to himself and chewed on his unlit cigar. I had fallen asleep in both À Bout de Souffle *and* Pierrot le Fou.

'One good thing you could say about him, he's worked with some beautiful women! He's made more films than I have and he started twenty years later.'

He relit his cigar.

'That's one thing people get right in Europe. They make films for reasonable budgets, unlike Hollywood where money is the only object. Those Hollywood guys have got themselves a good racket and they'll milk it for all it's worth. Who wouldn't? It's foolish men like me who can't see where art ends and business begins.'

Ann Rogers was a tweedy lady, like a large flightless bird, the then extinct Great Bustard, perhaps 60 years of age which, to my 22 years, seemed elderly. She was one of those people who had probably always been that age.

'People have ideal ages, don't they? Young men who will be more comfortable in their fifties and pretty middle-aged women who clearly peaked when they were sixteen. You, Dorian, I suspect will be in your forties.'

I asked him what about himself and he laughed, 'Now. Now is always my ideal age though everyone tells me it was when I was in my twenties.'

'He's always gonna be young,' interjected Oja, 'young in mind.'

'And in heart,' he added, reaching over to take her hand.

Ann Rogers explained that she ran Mr Welles's business affairs in London. She lived in a large and comfortable apartment in Maida Vale, that discreet corner of London named after an even more discreet military victory won by the British over the French in Calabria in 1806. She was married to an Australian who hardly knew who the hell Orson Welles was and was more interested in beating the English at cricket or reminding us of their efforts at

Gallipoli. When I pointed out to him that far more British were killed on that godforsaken Turkish peninsula than antipodeans, he was affronted.

Mrs Rogers told me that 'Mr Welles' was filming in Yugoslavia and needed some essential supplies. With no more ado, she handed me a large bundle of £50 notes, probably more cash than I had ever seen in my life before, and instructed me to go to two places in central London: the headquarters of Kodak in Covent Garden to buy ten 400ft rolls of 35mm film and Alfred Dunhill in Jermyn Street to buy 100 No. 1 Montecristo Havana cigars. These were the 'essential supplies' for 'Mr Welles,' as she called him.

Nothing else, just film and cigars! Something from Cuba, something from the USA – very Orson Welles, I thought. I liked it.

She also gave me enough cash to buy two top-of-the-range suitcases to house the film stock and the cigars. Her instructions were crisp and matter of fact and suited her tweed suit. I imagined her working for the Special Operations Executive in the war, efficiently sending agents off on deadly missions, many of them never to return. Or at Bletchley Park, valiantly typing up incomprehensible documents for shabby-suited academics with minds filled with numbers, codes and mathematical formulae. England seems to breed ladies like Mrs Rogers in abundance, whose driving force is duty, duty and then duty.

The next day, it was November I remember, I flew out of a grey, overcast and rainy London on a Jugoslav Aero Transport Caravelle to the Adriatic port of Split, the Roman and Venetian Spalato, where the Emperor Diocletian had built his great palace, grew cabbages, and gently debauched himself far away from prying Roman eyes.

As time passed in mid-air, I remember thinking Dr Johnson was quite wrong. I was bored with London. Well, at least with the verbosely named London School of Film Technique, a disused Victorian warehouse in Covent Garden, a far cry from the elegant quadrangles and colonnades of Oxford, where the fruit and vegetable market still ruled the roost.

The school was run by the pretentious, cheap-cigar-smoking Robert Dunbar who, having failed to achieve anything of worth in the movie industry, was making a living by overcharging naïve young would-be film-makers with disorganised lectures, random courses and out-of-date equipment. He was the epitome of the Oscar Wilde aphorism about teachers.

Unbeknownst to me, he was also a keen advocate of the dreaded ACTT, the Association of Cinematograph, Television and Allied Technicians, the trade union which was the Stasi of the British film industry. To work you had to have an ACTT card, but you couldn't get a card without a job and you couldn't get a job without a card. This resulted in a huge amount of nepotism in the business, where families tended to follow each other into particular professions. I had no family connections, but through one contact managed to get an interview with the head of production at Shepperton Studios.

I told some pathetic story of how I had run my school film society with screenings of *Citizen Kane* and other classic films. On one occasion, I had even organised a trip to Shepperton during the filming of *Becket* and had watched Richard Burton and Peter O'Toole on the set. Thinking back, my approach was pretty lame. This man was a technician and operative disinterested in the idea that film was art. For him, as with most technicians in the industry, it was a business, a technical business, like working in a factory. I subscribed more to the Mr Welles school of film-making: he told me he'd learnt all he needed to learn about the workings of a film camera in two days with Greg Toland.

Anyway, the Shepperton man told me that if I could get an ACTT card on the recommendation of Robert Dunbar, he would give me a job in production. It was a chicken and egg situation. Suffice it to say that my request to the seedy Dunbar was turned down on the grounds that, if he gave me a card, then he would have to give one to every other student. Since most of them were foreign nationals, I didn't see this as a problem and went away disappointed.

The ACTT was one of those ineffective trade unions where most of its members were permanently unemployed so the notion that it protected them was a nonsense. It fought back against movie producers by insisting on the most ridiculous crewing requirements. For example, four men were stipulated on a camera crew: the lighting cameraman or director of photography, the first assistant cameraman or camera operator, the second assistant cameraman or focus puller, and finally the third assistant cameraman or clapper boy, who loaded the 35mm magazines and operated the clapper board. This was fine on a major film, but on low-budget productions it was simply not necessary. Overtime was strictly adhered to, so the rules of the factory floor were implemented in film-making, which never made a lot of sense to me. The cars of film crews, when they turned up for work in film studios, were very top of the range – no struggling artists here, just hardnosed technicians like expensive electricians or plumbers.

The film school was a massive disappointment, a far cry from the wit and repartee of university, full of American Vietnam draft-dodgers, melodramatic Italians with no talent, boring Swiss, pretentious Iranian wannabes with nothing better to do with their lives, numerous left-orientated students and a myriad of other deadbeats. After the effete delights of Oxford, it was a huge comedown.

The one highlight for us men was a magnificent Israeli by the name of Osnat Krasnansky. She had served with the Israeli Army during the 1967 war and a bunch of unhealthy-looking film students were no worthy opponents for her when she had personally captured a whole unit of Egyptian infantry in the Sinai single-handed. With her tanned skin, her shining white teeth, her black tresses, black eyes and the body of an Olympic athlete, she was a girl apart.

Another singular person I met there was a tall, lugubrious young man named Robert Mrazek, a Cornell-educated American who had volunteered for service in Vietnam and had become an officer in the US Navy. Unfortunately, he had been partially blinded in a gunnery accident and sported a black patch over his injured eye like Nelson. We would compare notes most evenings in his dimly lit and dank flat overlooking the Thames in Pimlico, normally beginning with an earnest discussion on the early works of Lubitsch and Bergman, followed by enthusiastic slagging off of our fellow students, then further earnest discussions about our mutual heroes, President Kennedy, Horatio Nelson and, of course, the unattainable Osnat Krasnansky.

The few memorable moments at the school were lectures with Charles Frend, the director of *Scott of the Antarctic* and *The Cruel Sea*, talks by Roger Manvell, the first director of the British Film Academy, on the Nazi film propaganda machine, and an illuminating appearance from two young Czech directors, Ivan Passer and Milos Forman, recently escaped from Russian-occupied Prague. I had seen Forman's first film, *Loves of a Blonde*, a charming and funny black and white movie. He and Passer told harrowing stories about their difficulties under the Russian occupation. A few weeks later, Forman went to Hollywood and went on to direct a number of films, including *One Flew Over the Cuckoo's Nest* and *Amadeus*.

'I turned up at the Gate Theatre in Dublin and told them I was a Broadway star. I was sixteen, I think. They gave me a star part in their next production. So, I started as a star and I've been working my way down ever since!'

2

BALKAN DISCUSSIONS

I was met at Split airport by a Yugoslav youth, Mirko, who chain-smoked the strong local Sava cigarettes, drove me to a small fishing village a little way up the coast called Primošten and installed me in the completely deserted hotel, the only one in town. It wasn't quite the Bates Motel, but not far off, a sort of Mediterranean version of the hotel in *The Shining* with a hint of the Iron Curtain about it. Commissars from Hungary and middle-ranking Stasi agents from East Germany doubtless summered there with their fat, ill-dressed wives.

'Do you want to rest, or what?' Mirko asked me abruptly.

Holding up the enormously heavy suitcase, I suggested we go and tell Mr Welles that his goods had arrived. We proceeded down to the little port with its leisure boats wrapped up in canvas covers for the winter and drove along the deserted jetty towards what was evidently a small film crew, who were working on the deck of a large yacht.

I got out of the car in the fading Mediterranean light and approached. There was a cold breeze blowing, making the halyards rattle against the unused masts. Orson Welles stood on the yacht holding onto the mast for stability.

There was no doubt it was Orson Welles. He was enormous, tall, broad, all in black with a black cloak and a black hat, very much the magician, which, of course, he was.

★

'Cinematography is a form of conjuring. Interiors may be in a studio while the exteriors may be an amalgam of completely different locations. A doorway out of one room leads you to a location 1,000 miles away but it looks real. The audience have been tricked. Nothing is what it seems.'

★

I had seen hundreds of black and white photographs of him, and there he was, the man himself standing alone on a borrowed yacht in a deserted harbour on a little-visited coastline.

His film crew were huddled below decks when I arrived, presumably attempting to stay out of the biting wind. People think it never gets cold in the Mediterranean. Believe me, it does. I have to repeat here I was not a very tall young man and Orson Welles was a very big man in every sense of the word, a big presence with a big black cloak and a big black hat and a big deep voice. You get the picture?

'Mr Welles?' I asked, knowing perfectly well to whom I spoke, 'I've brought your cigars and film stock.'

That was the first time I ever addressed him. I called him 'Mr Welles,' as Mrs Rogers did. For me it was a sign of respect from a young man to an older man. But it was not just that. It was more. I did respect him, genuinely. And I wanted to reinforce it to him, so he understood where I stood with him. Not subservient, but junior to him. It always bugged me when people of all ages who'd known him for five minutes called him 'Orson.' I suppose it's a little old-fashioned, but there it is and he accepted it. Although we were in a theatrical world, we had both been brought up old-style and that was the way.

I stood still, waiting for the real-life Orson Welles to speak his unforgettable first words to me. I have to repeat them, I enjoy them so much.

'Yes,' he said, 'you must be Dorian St George Bond. With a name like that you've just gotta be a movie director!' With that, he roared with laughter and the crew chuckled in unison. He then told me to go back to the hotel and wait for him.

As historic meetings go, this one obviously doesn't rank very highly in the scheme of things. I never met Dr Livingstone in Africa or the Duke of Wellington after the Battle of Waterloo. I was certainly no Henry Morton Stanley or Marshal Blücher. But it was historic for me, and it had the format of importance in that we both instantly knew who the other man was. I cherish it to this day.

So, I sat in the deserted, white summer lobby of the Dalmatian hotel and waited nervously for the great man. Maybe he would just take the cigars and Kodak and say, 'thank you and goodbye.' At least I would get a night on the Dalmatian coast, albeit in winter when all the bars and restaurants were closed, before returning to London.

After about an hour, Welles and his mini-entourage swept in. He immediately began talking to me in the most charming manner: How was my flight? Had I been to Yugoslavia before?

This was my moment. I considered myself an expert on Yugoslavia. I told Mr Welles that, yes, I had been to Yugoslavia on a number of occasions before, and in fact my stepmother was a Serbian émigrée whose father had been court jeweller in Belgrade to the charismatic King Peter I of Serbia before the First World War. The king had regaled him with stories of his military exploits. He had fought with the French Foreign Legion during the Franco-Prussian War, been wounded at Orléans, and only managed to escape the Prussians by swimming across the Loire.

Milan Stojesiljevic and his young wife, parents to my beloved stepmother and her brother, had succumbed to influenza in the great outbreak of 1919, leaving their two infant children as orphans. I rattled on with the tale of how the two children survived their privileged but lonely childhoods, with Katerina being brought up by maiden aunts and Nikola attending boarding school followed by military academy, how she married, very young, an equally young heir to a mercantile fortune who died shortly thereafter of tuberculosis. By this time, I was getting quite carried away, telling Mr Welles that I loved the Serbs who had been our Allies in both the Great War and the Second World War and that I hated the Croats, many of whom had served in the SS and had killed more than a million Serbs in concentration camps.

He seemed amused by my outburst, and smiled mischievously. When I finally drew breath, he coolly introduced me to a tall, striking-looking young woman in her mid- to late twenties who was watching me stonily. She had a strong Slavonic face with a hint of Mongolian origins from centuries ago. 'This is Olga Palinkaš and she is a Croat.'

'Call me Oja,' she smiled menacingly at me through her perfect white teeth. 'We're all Croats here.'

I mumbled a pathetic apology, while Mr Welles enjoyed the moment and roared with laughter. 'You're in the Balkans here, boy, so beware!'

I later discovered Oja's father was Hungarian, so I felt a little better. Over tea, they told me how they had first met in Zagreb in 1962 when Welles was shooting Kafka's *The Trial*. Oja told me that she was studying at the School of Fine Arts and had been out with a friend of her parents at the legendary Esplanade Hotel. In the bar, her friend had suddenly said to her, 'Orson Welles, the famous film director, is sitting right behind you. Don't look.' Of course, she looked, only to be confronted by a lot of indoor palms, behind which was the instantly recognisable Mr Welles.

'She was so beautiful that I came right across to talk to her. And that was it.'

'Well, not quite!' said Oja, 'A few things happened in between.'

'You tell him the story, I enjoy hearing it.'

'So we talked for ages and ages at the bar. Mainly about art. Then you invited me to watch the filming and told me you would send a car for me in the morning.'

'Always, a gentleman,' breathed Mr Welles.

'And, sure enough, the car duly arrived. A big car, and there were hardly any cars in that area outside Zagreb at that time! So, all my neighbours were looking. And at the location I was very embarrassed because when I walked in everybody stopped and looked at me.'

'You were so beautiful.'

'I met Tony Perkins, Orson's big friend, and all the others.'

'It was grand.' Mr Welles was getting a little bored with the story now and was looking about the room.

'And that was how it all started?' I asked.

'Yup,' grunted Mr Welles.

'Not exactly, my love,' Oja laughed, 'You never called me. You just left Zagreb and never called. I didn't know what to do. I was very upset by you.'

'I'm sorry,' he exhaled. 'We had to leave. The local production company were overcharging grotesquely and there was no way we could pay. The Salkinds had run out of money. The Zagreb people thought they had us over a barrel, so we just left town.'

'It was two years later. I was in Paris studying fine arts. I lived in a little garret on the Faubourg St Antoine. Right at the top.'

'And I found you. And I walked right up and broke down your door when you refused to open it to me!'

'And that was it. We fell in love.'

'Wow,' I said.

With that, Welles bade me good evening and told me to meet him for breakfast at 5.30 the following morning.

It occurred to me that this was a case of the comfort of strangers. I was a stranger, or at least a new kid on the block, and they could tell me this pretty intimate story with impunity. I would be gone in a few days and who could I tell?

Weeks later, when Oja could see me thinking about their age difference, she quickly dispelled my image of the old fading film director with the young budding actress. 'He's the youngest-spirited guy I've ever met, fun, loving, imaginative, mischievous, everything. The idea he's old is ridiculous. Very often he's younger than me.'

The Yugoslav youth, Mirko, also a Croat (after all, we were in Croatia), asked if I'd like to eat with his family. I was thankful for the invitation, since the hotel restaurant had the look of a communist canteen, and went with him to a fisherman's house where we were cooked fresh sardines and drank Dalmatian wine. I wondered whether Raymond of Toulouse and his fellow Crusaders had eaten half this well as they trudged down this desolately beautiful coastline a thousand years before me. After all, Diocletian had lived happily here for a number of years in his retirement.

I slept nervously, wondering whether I would be sent back to the shoddy realities of film school, with its smell of rotting cabbages, the following day. Diocletian again.

★

'Did you know that one of the best places to buy Cuban cigars in the world is Communist China? The two Communist brother countries find their trade a little imbalanced and the only thing the Cubans can offer to them is their cigars, that ultimate symbol of the capitalist world.'

'They should name a cigar after you,' I ventured. 'After all, there's a Churchill.'

'Churchill was Churchill,' Mr Welles growled, before taking another puff. 'He came round to my dressing room once in London when I was playing Macbeth. He quoted one of my speeches, then continued on into the rest of the speech which I had cut out to make the play less tediously long! He didn't miss a trick!

'I'll tell you a funny story. He was out of power then. Having presided over one of the most important events in world history alongside dear old FDR, he lost the election. I suppose rightly. He was a little out of date by then, a man who had charged at Omdurman against the Fuzzy Wuzzies. Anyway, I was in Venice on the Lido trying to persuade an expatriate Russian Armenian to put up some money for me for a movie I'd written. As we walked through the hotel lobby to lunch, Churchill was standing there with Clemmie and we

nodded to each other. At lunch the Russian was suitably impressed. Actually, he wasn't just impressed, he was bowled over! How on earth did I know one of the architects of the Allied victory in 1945?

'*The next day I was swimming opposite the hotel and suddenly found myself near Churchill.*

'"*Mr Churchill," I said, "I have to thank you for acknowledging me yesterday. The man I was with is being pursued by me to invest in a film I plan to make. He thinks I am very well connected."*

'"*Little does he know that I am no longer Prime Minister. Russians are not familiar with our democratic systems!"*

'*With that, he swam away and joined Clemmie on the beach.*

'*That evening, as I walked into dinner with my Russian friend, we passed Mr Churchill's table. Without hesitation, Churchill stood up and bowed deeply as I passed.*'

Mr Welles enacted the bow and we roared with laughter. Here was one of the most famous actors in the world charmingly re-enacting a scene from his past when probably the most famous man in the world had bowed to him in jest. A wonderful moment for me.

I told Mr Welles some days later that I had attended Churchill's lying-in-state in Westminster Hall in January 1965, and with all the other people of England had shuffled past his coffin illuminated by four great candles and bowed my head. The next day I had stood in the grey January day and watched his coffin go by on a gun carriage and felt this was truly a marker of the end of empire, the end of Britain as a world power.

'*Did you know Churchill ran most of the war drunk on cognac? That's why he got along so well with that old rogue Stalin! Poor FDR was most disapproving.*'

I then told him the Churchill Yalta story. At the conference, the three world leaders would sit around the table with their aides. Notes were passed between them constantly as the talks progressed. One day, Churchill passed a note to Anthony Eden, his foreign secretary, which the Russians managed to retrieve from a wastepaper basket.

It read, 'Dead birds don't fall out of nests.'

Stalin was intrigued. Surely this was a code about some diabolical act the Allies were planning. For days the NKVD, the predecessors of the KGB, attempted to break the code. They failed. Stalin was at his wits' end. That evening after dinner, when he and Churchill were having a drink together, he asked the question.

'Mr Churchill, I have to ask you something. It's about a note you wrote to your aides some days ago. It said, 'Dead birds don't fall out of nests.'

'Oh, that,' smiled Churchill wryly.

'We are Allies, Mr Churchill, please enlighten me.'

Churchill took another mouthful of Cognac. 'It isn't a code, Secretary Stalin. It was a reply to a note from Mr Eden telling me my fly buttons were undone!'

3

SHADES OF 1968

'We skipped the light fandango, turned cartwheels across the floor, I was feeling kind of seasick …' The BBC's Radio 1 was blasting out 'A Whiter Shade of Pale' by Procol Harum which, a year before, had been the soundtrack to my final exams at Oxford. It made me feel a little bittersweet aware that those days had now gone and I was wondering where my life would take me. I sat in my car listening to the music playing for a long moment before getting out, filling up with petrol and going in to pay and buy a sandwich.

As I climbed back into my car, the track changed to the sophisticated sound of Dionne Warwick's 'Do you know the way to San Jose.' As she reached the line, 'LA is a great big freeway,' the programme was interrupted: 'We are getting news that Senator Robert Kennedy has been shot in Los Angeles.'

I froze in my seat and didn't move. The track continued, the DJ made some lame remark, and I flicked through the channels to find out more. The BBC News gave me the answer:

Bobby Kennedy, Senator Robert Kennedy, the front-runner for the Democratic nomination for president in the forthcoming US presidential election, has been shot and severely wounded. He was just leaving a Democratic victory celebration when he was shot. We will bring you more news as we receive it.

Five years before, as a schoolboy, I had heard about the assassination of President John F. Kennedy and watched dumbfounded as the events unfolded, from the sight of the bloodied Jacky Kennedy on the steps of Air Force One, to the chaotic swearing-in of Lyndon Johnson inside the aircraft, to the sombre funeral on the streets of Washington a few days later. It seemed the deaths of the two Kennedy brothers had bookended my time at university, along with the death of Winston Churchill – 1963, 1965 and now 1968.

Their rise to prominence had brought to an end the dreary era of my post-war childhood. They were young, good-looking, vigorous men with the dreams and ambitions that we all aspired to. They would be our leaders into the future, rather than the drab old men who had emerged after the war, many of whom were like our grandfathers. The Kennedys, with their glamorous wives and ways, were like our fathers. What we didn't know about were their antics with wild women like Marilyn Monroe, who had famously died the year before Jack Kennedy, a few weeks after singing 'Happy Birthday' to him in Madison Square Garden.

Now they were gone. The flame had died.

I returned to the set of the student documentary film I was directing about a recently released young criminal and his road to salvation. I had found him as a subject by contacting the probation service, who had been reluctant to become involved but had finally agreed. They gave me a young boy whom they considered safe for eager film students to work with. I liked him and he was very co-operative. What turned me off was the fact that he had been fostered out in his teenage years to the well-known playwright Robert Bolt, who had written, most famously, *A Man for all Seasons*. Some months later, after he had been moved again, he returned to Bolt's big house in Richmond and robbed him. Talk about biting the hand that feeds you. (*A Man for all Seasons* was a masterly stage play by Robert Bolt and a movie directed by Fred Zinnemann, who had made the immortal *High Noon*. Orson Welles played the part of Cardinal Wolsey.)

The next day in the film school, some clown was shouting about how the Kennedys were all capitalists anyway, and what were we looking depressed about? The school was permeated with political persuasions far to the Left. They say if you're not a Communist when you're 20, you have no heart, and if you're not a Conservative when you're 40, you're a fool. I must have had no heart in those days.

Anyway, that morning we had a lecture on 'Orson Welles and Shakespeare' and I was mesmerised by that shot in *Othello* where Micheál Mac Liammóir, as Iago, is hung in a cage above the battlements of what Mr Welles later told me was Mogador in Morocco. Unforgettable. And the bathhouse murder of Cassio? Brilliant.

'The costumes hadn't arrived from Italy. So we had to improvise. In a bathhouse you don't wear clothes, just nakedness and towels.'

I was transported into the real world of Shakespeare by means of the visual imagination of Orson Welles. What a gift he had. I can't think of any director who has had such a signature style: like an artist whose pictures you instantly recognise.

I sat in the darkness of the brick-walled lecture room and was transported to another world. Orson Welles was a master.

4

Hair Dyeing in the Adriatic

Breakfast the next morning, probably the earliest I had ever eaten it, was the forerunner of many meals with the great man, although I did not know it at the time. The three main protagonists were to be Mr Welles, Oja Palinkas and me. Everyone else had walk-on parts.

Picture an enormous man dressed all in black sitting uncomfortably away from a small table-clothed table, breathing audibly as he ate. Contrary to rumour, he did not eat vast amounts of food. He ate voraciously, yes, and always enjoyed the best – don't most of us do the same, given the chance? He was a connoisseur of food, with enormous knowledge on the subject, as with most things.

★

I was sucking down another mouthful of pasta al pomodoro when Mr Welles broke off from his vast starter of spaghetti alla vongole and turned to me. 'What's your favourite soup on a hot summer's day?'

'Gazpacho and then Vichyssoise,' I replied confidently.

'And where do they originate?'

This was clearly a trick question, but I blundered on. 'I suppose Spain and France.'

'Wrong, boy. Spain, Portugal and the United States. Vichyssoise was invented at the Ritz Carlton in New York by a wonderful chef

*I knew well called Diet. What a great name for a chef!' He roared
with laughter at his own joke. 'For God's sake, a chef called Diet.'*

'Seriously?' I questioned.

'I'm not kidding, his name was Louis Diat, pronounced Dia. He
was French. He was tall and elegant and had cooked for your King
Edward VII, that great bon viveur.'

I suddenly envisioned King Edward VII with Orson Welles: what
a perfect pair! Each with a fat cigar in their hand and each replete
with a belly full of an over-rich dinner drowned in rich red wine
from the most exclusive château vineyards in Bordeaux.

'And me, he cooked for me as a parvenu on Broadway when I was
a young man. He was trained and elevated by Monsieur Ritz and
Monsieur Escoffier himself. In terms of pedigree, you don't get better
than that. He was one of the best.'

'So, it is a French invention.'

'No, it was invented by a Frenchman who came from somewhere
near Vichy, in New York when he was a naturalised American.
I therefore claim it as American!'

I was not going to argue about something as trivial as potato soup
with a few onions in it. I lapped down the rest of the tomato soup
and began to think that maybe, after all, it took the gold medal before
Gazpacho and Vichyssoise.

Soup, be it cold and refreshing in the summer or warm and reas-
suring in the winter, is a much-underestimated thing. Come to think
of it, for thousands of years it's been common food for most people,
alongside gruel or porridge or some kind of solid stew or soup. Meat
would be a luxury, a chanced-upon deer or an ageing chicken long
past its sell-by date.

★

History, politics, current affairs and travel were covered that
morning, as they were most days, interspersed with throwaway
lines of devastating accuracy or intimacy about some major figure
of the twentieth century that he had had dealings with.

'Houdini was a rough diamond. A good man, though. After he died, Beatrice, his wife, spent years waiting for a message from him from the other side. Like the Empress Eugenie with her son Napoleon, the Prince Imperial, after he was killed in the Zulu War. She even travelled to the site in Natal where he had died,' I added and, for a brief moment, Mr Welles looked interested.

There was little he didn't know about, and little he wouldn't talk about.

'Larry Olivier was pretty dim, you know. A fine actor but not a lot going on inside that skull of his. Actors in general don't need to be smart. In fact, an empty vessel is the best thing. Most actors are hollow. The joke is that the media somehow persuade the outside that they are profound or meaningful, when in fact they are just a bunch of chancers who get paid too much money and never own up to it. Have you ever seen an actor or actress tell a chat show host what they earned on their last picture? But they're quick to foist their political opinions on anyone who will listen, as if they are the only inhabitants of the moral high ground. It's easy to be on the high ground when you are rich and privileged and distant from the banalities of the real world.'

The mechanics of film-making bored him: 'I am a story teller, an entertainer. How I do it is of no interest to me. Are you telling me people would ask Leonardo how he did his sketches? Or what paper Michelangelo chose to paint on, for God's sake? What you do or create is what is important. How you do it has now become an obsession with small-brained critics who have nothing better to do than analyse rather than do!

'Doctors don't come home and talk endlessly about their patients, in fact they're not allowed to. It's the same with lawyers. There's little more boring than directors, and certainly actors, droning on about how they did this or that, which is probably a lie anyway!'

He roared with laughter and I silently agreed with him.

'Can you imagine Rembrandt talking about how he applied his paintbrush to canvas? He might as well have talked about paint drying!' Another guffaw. 'Well, he would have been talking about paint drying.' A long exhalation.

'If we are talking about chiaroscuro, then Caravaggio, I prefer,' he growled. 'He was a murderer, you know. His story would make a great movie. All filmed in his type of lighting. He killed a man after losing a game of indoor tennis. He'd probably lost money on a bet as well. He stabbed him in the groin. Can you imagine the blood spreading across the sanded floor of the court, Caravaggio's escaping footprints in the blood, his flight through the back streets of Rome?'

Mr Welles was very much a gentleman and gentlemen don't, as a rule, talk about their work or themselves unless specifically questioned. For some reason that first morning, we got onto the topic of the dazzling but flawed Gabriele D'Annunzio: 'Some of his poetry is the most sensual I have ever read in any language and he was a very brave man. He actually flew across the Dolomites in an open aeroplane and dropped handheld bombs onto Vienna during the First World War. And he claimed to be the world's greatest cunnilingus artist.'

Mr Welles breathed out again and smiled. He gazed across at Oja and she met him with a stony stare. I nervously reached for my empty coffee cup:

'When I first went to England, I wasn't even twenty. I went and looked up George Bernard Shaw. I took a taxi out to his house in Hertfordshire somewhere and just introduced myself. I'd come from the Abbey Theatre in Dublin and he knew Micheál Mac Liammóir and Hilton. What a playwright! I put on *Captain Courageous* some years later, but all he wanted to do was talk politics. It was the time of the Depression. He said something to me that I've never forgotten. He told me that all politicians were abnormal, given that it is not normal to have a desire to order other people how to live their lives.'

With that pearl of wisdom from the man who had written that masterpiece *Saint Joan*, and spoken by the man who had played the part of Charles Foster Kane, the meal was at an end. Mr Welles pushed his chair back and stood up. I noticed what dainty little black lace-up shoes he had supporting his giant body.

'I'll see you down at the dock.'

'Yes,' I said.

I don't exactly recall all the other words spoken at that breakfast, but I do remember we had talked more politics than film. In fact, nothing about film which, in fact, is a rather tedious subject anyway. You either do it or you don't, but you don't talk about it. The amusing parts come in between, as I was soon to find out.

I followed him and Oja down to the deserted harbour decorated by the many-coloured canvases which buttoned up the hibernating yachts. The film crew consisted of three, including the director of photography, Tomislav Pinter, and his two assistants, Novak and Branko.

Branko was permanently unshaven, long before it became fashionable, and had no front teeth, always noticeable since he spent a lot of time grinning from ear to ear. Having trouble with a slow puncture on the camera vehicle, he removed the tyre, laid it on the ground and flattened the rim with a formidable hammer. He looked up at me and grinned, '*Teknik Yugoslavische!*' I dread to think what he would have done to German prisoners in the war. He had been a Chetnik. I'll explain who they were later in my story.

Pinter, probably the most eminent Yugoslav cameraman of his time, had been the director of photography on the epic film *The Battle of Neretva*, a Yugoslav production extolling the heroism of President Tito, starring Yul Brynner, Hardy Kruger, Curt Jurgens, Franco Nero and Orson Welles, among others, including Sergei Bondarchuk, of whom more later.

Marshal Tito, real name Josip Broz, had personally signed off on the enormous budget of the film. Mr Welles pointed out to me how clever Tito was never to claim a particular tribal connection, Slovenian, Croatian or Serbian, so he could maintain his impartial and iron grip on that now disparate country.

He told me the story of how Tito had been a man of mystery during the war. Evelyn Waugh, one of the Brits dropped into

Yugoslavia along with Fitzroy Maclean and Randolph Churchill, was always convinced that Tito was a woman.

Waugh had once met Tito on the Dalmatian coast, Tito had approached in very brief swimwear, his manhood clearly visible, and asked, 'I gather, Major Waugh, you think I'm a woman?'

'And another thing,' Mr Welles continued. 'Did you know he's the only Communist leader alive who actually took part in the Russian Revolution?'

★

The day was crisp and clear as Mr Welles stepped aboard the yacht they were filming on. For such a large man, he moved pretty daintily. Not quite a dancer, but certainly a surefooted actor. I waited on the dock, not sure what to do.

'Come on board,' Mr Welles called, and I leapt onto the deck.

His request was not a request. It was an order. That was fine by me, as I was just thinking of deferring the moment I would be dispensed with and sent back to a dreary winter in London.

There was a stiff breeze blowing and it was quite difficult keeping your footing on the moving deck of the narrow yacht. I began to worry how I was going get out of the way when they started filming. Mr Welles was peering through the viewfinder of his 35mm French Cameflex Éclair camera for his familiar impossible angles. Not many people, even top directors, owned their own 35mm movie camera in those days and I was impressed. By taking off the magazine, he was able to use the skeleton of the camera as a viewfinder since it was light and wieldy.

Mirko produced a shotgun to be a used as a prop for Mr Welles when his character bludgeoned someone with the twin barrels. No one seemed to know how to dismantle the weapon. This was my moment. I took the gun and 'broke' it into its three component parts, handing Mr Welles the barrels to be used as a bludgeon. He was impressed at something that most boys brought up in the countryside in England know by heart. I had won myself a stay of execution!

I had learnt from the crew that Mr Welles was doing some pick-up shots that he needed for his half-finished film, *The Deep*, which was adapted from the Charles Williams thriller *Dead Calm*. With the working title of 'Dead Reckoning,' about skulduggery off the Skeleton Coast of south-west Africa, it starred Orson Welles, Olga Palinkas, Michael Bryant, Laurence Harvey and Jeanne Moreau. Welles had written the script and was financing it himself.

★

'I don't want to make it an art house movie. That's why I've shot it in colour. It's the first film where my main intention is to make money. It's a commercial exercise with commercially viable actors. We'll get there in the end.'

★

The film was never finished, and to this day still languishes some-where in some film vault. Oja later sold the book rights to an Australian company, who made the 1983 version with Nicole Kidman and Sam Neill.

Next morning, Welles looked at me closely at the breakfast table and, nodding to Oja, said, 'Yes, he'll be fine.'

Fine for what? I thought.

'Dorian, I want you to double for Michael Bryant in a shot for me.'

'OK,' I said eagerly. At that moment, and most subsequent moments, I would have jumped off a cliff for him.

'There's just one thing, Michael is blonde, so we'll have to get your hair dyed.'

'No problem,' I replied enthusiastically, not realising the ramifications of the fact that Mr Welles was somewhat keen on changing the hair colour of his artists – for example, Marlene Dietrich in *Touch of Evil*, Rita Hayworth in *The Lady from Shanghai* and now me in 'Dead Reckoning,' aka *The Deep*. I was in good company!

Michael Bryant was a prominent English actor at that time who had played Lenin in the movie *Nicholas and Alexandra*. He bore a striking resemblance to the leader of the Russian Revolution. Some years later, when shooting a TV commercial in Moscow for Procter and Gamble, I had a flashback to Michael Bryant. The fading Russian actress playing the housewife was continually fluffing her lines, and the director complained to me that he couldn't make any headway with her. I approached her on the set and at once realised she was stone drunk on vodka. Through an interpreter, I asked her politely to get her act together. This did not go down well. She drew herself up to her full height, which probably reached my chin.

'Do you know who I am?' she demanded.

I shrugged my shoulders in ignorance.

'My name is Inna Ivanovna Ulianova.'

'And?' I foolishly replied.

'Uli-ano-va,' she repeated slowly, annunciating each syllable.

Then the penny dropped. 'Ulianov' was Lenin's name. And she was a member of his family, a Communist aristocrat by any measure. And here I was, slap-bang in the middle of Communist Russia, where their greatest hero was Lenin. He of the death masked face, lying in his mausoleum outside the walls of the forbidding Kremlin, looking seriously like Michael Bryant.

'Ulianova,' I announced. 'Wow, that's serious.'

I didn't know whether to laugh or be afraid. It transpired that she was the niece of the notorious man. Ulianova just sneered at my ignorance and, with a dismissive wave of her arm, tottered off to her dressing room for another swig of her vodka bottle. Suffice it to say, we finished the filming very late that night.

Mr Welles summoned Mirko and asked if he knew a hair stylist. Mirko knew just the place. In his clapped-out Lada, we sped to the local town of Šibenik, or Sebenico to the Venetians, replete with the winged lion of St Mark above its Renaissance gates.

Whatever hairstyling had been like in 1768, it had certainly gone backwards by 1968. With the use of strong chemicals, the kind that polluted most of the rivers and lakes of Eastern Europe during that period, my hair was turned a luminescent yellow. The peroxide was administered by a strongly forearmed Croat lady, who had probably personally castrated any unfortunate German stragglers during the war.

I am not joking.

I had met Field Marshal Lord Harding the previous year. The much decorated and many times wounded grand old man, a veteran of the battles of Gallipoli, Gaza, Tobruk and El Alamein, Monte Cassino and the Gothic Line, had ended the war as commander of XIII Corps in the spring of 1945 in Trieste. There, his army had met up with Tito's partisans on the Italian border as the Germans surrendered. Getting out of his jeep to meet Marshal Tito, he told me the most terrifying soldiers he had ever met in his life were Tito's personal bodyguard of Amazon-like partisan women, brandishing weaponry of all shapes and sizes and bristling with naked aggression. 'Their forearms were like the thighs of athletes, their fingers on the triggers of their weapons, thick black hair, not quite moustaches but not far off. I would not like to have met them in hand-to-hand fighting.' This remark came from a man who was not prone to hyperbole. Whoever said old soldiers were boring?

The feeling on the crown of my head, as the peroxide was poured on, was akin to the feeling of vinegar being poured onto an open wound, a burning pain that spread across my skull like some awful futuristic poison from a low-budget Roger Corman film.

After my hair had dried and was suitably coiffured, Mirko and the woman whispered to each other and roared with laughter when he'd slipped her the necessary recompense. She pulled out a filterless cigarette and lit it, blowing the smoke at me. She said something crude, clearly along the lines of the supposition that I was gay and would have better luck with the boys with this new look. I was not too happy with their mockery and walked off in a sulk, telling Mirko to pick me up in an hour.

I ambled into the old town and found myself in front of the exquisite cathedral of St James. It was a Renaissance masterpiece, built by Venetian masons with the local white marble from Brač. I entered through a great door guarded by the requisite two Venetian stone lions. Inside, it was more grey than white, illuminated by a clear glass rose window, the tall windows behind the altar and the cupola windows above. Horizontal metal stays ensured the verticality of the ancient pillars that formed the nave – pillars which, I sensed, came from another incarnation 1,000 years before when Diocletian ruled this coast and tried to turn back the incoming tide of Christianity. I knelt and prayed that I could work for Mr Welles forever.

The next morning Mr Welles and Oja were delighted with the result of my new hairstyle when I met them for breakfast. I told them about my torturer and how she reminded me of the Field Marshal Harding story, which Mr Welles liked and Oja didn't. She looked confused, thinking I was insulting Yugoslav females. It was never clear to me what side her family had been on during the war. All I know is the Croats produced an SS division, thousands of recruits into the *Wehrmacht*, and a brutally efficient concentration camp. Like the French who, after 6 June 1944, all joined the Resistance, so, as the tide turned, I suspect many Croats fell into line behind Tito and the Allies.

After putting a nautical cap on me as well as the wardrobe jacket worn by Michael Bryant, we proceeded down to Primošten harbour and cast off in the yacht. We headed out to sea, where we were going to film, and I noticed there was quite a swell. The small rubber dinghy we were towing was hauled in close and Mr Welles told me to get in and take the oars. No problem, I thought, as I stepped in and, as is nautical custom, immediately sat down. No problem.

I was to be accompanied in the rubber dinghy by Tomislav, who was going to sit behind me and shoot over my shoulder. No problem.

Now, here's the thing. A very large American movie star by the name of Orson Welles was going to join us in the tiny dinghy. I looked at the dinghy, then at Mr Welles, and feared for all our safety. The water was freezing and by now was quite choppy. As I've explained already, Mr Welles was not of normal proportions. He was big, by any standards.

I took the measly little oars and steadied myself, edging the little craft nearer to the yacht which, by now, was virtually towering over me. This obviously encouraged Mr Welles who now boldly stepped down into the dinghy in front of me. The problem was, he didn't sit down immediately and you know the old adage about standing up in small boats – and this wasn't a small boat, it was a *tiny* dinghy. I couldn't control the tilting of the craft and I didn't want to drown in some deserted Yugoslav fishing village in the middle of winter.

'It's better if you sit down right away, Mr Welles,' I squeaked nervously, and he did exactly that.

I know he had played Captain Ahab some time ago and, like Moby Dick, he collapsed into the puny seat of the dinghy, making it settle even deeper into the water but at the same time sort of stabilising itself. Archimedes himself ruminating in Syracuse would have had some thoughts on water displacement if he had witnessed us.

'Let's go,' said Mr Welles, and I rowed away from the yacht.

The shot we were after was a close-up of Mr Welles with the back of my blonde head in the foreground. Simple really, except that it was November and, as I've said, the water was extremely choppy. Every swelling wave threatened to capsize us as I rowed round in slow circles to accommodate Mr Welles. They always say never film on boats since you are always moving and you have to adjust your position to the sun.

Finally, the camera turned long enough, and after a number of takes Mr Welles was happy. He was never one to hesitate about whether he had a shot or not. He was decisive and didn't hang about. He knew what he wanted and how it would look.

'Anybody can be a director, but to be a good one is a different matter. Every jumped-up actor, cameraman or editor. The sad truth is that they simply promote themselves to their levels of incompetence and we lose them as excellent technicians. There's many a great camera-man and great editor who has become a mediocre director.'

I precariously rowed back to the yacht and watched as Pinter and Mr Welles clambered back aboard. Pinter later whispered to me that he couldn't swim but he hadn't had the courage to tell Mr Welles! Our combined weights could probably have sunk the dinghy on a calm day, but we managed, somehow.

Mr Welles told me that he liked being the master of his own film-making. Like a painter in his studio, he would work on different canvases as the mood took him. Often film projects were discarded for months, even years on end. When I was with him, he had about four projects underway, not to speak of his acting roles. He let rip about Irving Thalberg, among others, 'the new moguls,' who consid-ered themselves arbiters of taste whereas the originals such as Harry Cohen, who founded Columbia Pictures, Sam Goldwyn, and the Warner brothers had been New York corner boys who were in it for the money and sometimes let creative talent blossom.

'It was Thalberg who created the modern idea of the all-powerful producer. They never existed before his appearance. There were just film-makers who found backers and studios to work with. He was the original monster, that ghastly spectre, the Creative Producer. Now Hollywood is crawling with them, power-crazed boys from Brooklyn determined to impose their will on us poor directors and writers. Thank God he wasn't still around when I got to Hollywood.'

★

At the end of six days, as we walked into the hotel in the late afternoon, Mr Welles told me that we would be leaving the next day.

The next morning standing in the hotel lobby, I was priming myself to say thank you to him and goodbye. He strode past me down the hotel steps to his waiting taxi, then turned and said, 'Goodbye, Dorian.' Before the driver closed his door, he looked back at me. 'Do you want to work for me?'

'That would be great,' I stuttered.

'Then call me when you get back to London.'

Exactly the words I had wanted to hear. He topped this by collapsing into the back of the Split taxi and saying to the astonished driver, 'Take me to Milan.'

I should point out to some of you whose geography is not brilliant that, although Spalato, as it was known to Italians, had been part of the Venetian Empire in the eighteenth century, it was now slap-bang in the middle of Yugoslavia, more than 500 miles from Milan. Nevertheless, off the taxi went without any hesitation. I can only assume the driver had his passport with him and that he is now a rich man! Later, in Rome, someone told me he had taken a similar journey from Rome to the South of France for a farewell assignation with Rita Hayworth. Apparently, their assignation was not a success and a few days later she married Prince Ali Khan.

I flew that evening from Split to Belgrade, and as the Douglas DC-4 droned through the cold night air above a moonlit and snow-covered Bosnia, I wondered what lay in store for me. Whatever would come to pass, I had had an unforgettable week.

★

Belgrade was a good place for a short break with some old Serbian friends including Milica, my Serbian uncle's daughter, and the exotic and effete Lazar Šecerovic, who lived in a faded palazzo decorated with elaborate cornices and heavy gilt-framed Old Masters, or paintings claiming to be Old Masters.

They had all heard of Orson Welles. They were in awe of him. But they were somewhat bemused by my blonde hair until I explained. We talked of two summers past when we had swum across the fast-flowing Sava River at its confluence with the Danube and the migrating storks high in their thick nests in the poplar trees had watched us like Byzantine sentries. Nine hundred years before, the lantern-jawed Peter the Hermit and his fanatical followers had struggled across these self-same waters in the face of strangely chain-mailed soldiers loyal to an emperor far away in Constantinople.

From there we had followed the ancient paths of the Crusaders across the Balkans, into Asia Minor and through Syria all the way to the gates of Jerusalem. Now my journey had no set path or plan, but I knew how I wanted it to go. If Mr Welles were a crusading knight errant then I would willingly be his squire. Sir Orson Welles certainly had a ring to it. Or maybe it was more Don Quixote and Sancho Panza.

The only problem would have been getting him onto his horse, like Henry VIII in his later years.

★

'If Churchill was half-American, what about Stalin being a Georgian, Alexander the Great a Yugoslav, Hitler an Austrian, Napoleon an Italian, the Duke of Wellington an Irishman, the Buddha an Indian and Jesus Christ a Jew? By the way, most of them were short, very short. Tito was short and Mussolini. What is it with short men, Dorian, can you tell me? What is your problem?'

These off-the-cuff observations were normally terminated with an exhalation of cigar smoke and a teasing chuckle.

'Are you an outsider?' I asked. 'An American in Europe and yet a sort of European in America?'

Mr Welles pulled the wet cigar out of his mouth and considered for a moment.

'A lot of people think you're English.'

'Hell, no. I'm not sure whether that is a compliment or not? But I'll settle for the land which produced William Shakespeare and Joseph Conrad.'

'He was a Pole. Another man of no fixed homeland.'

'I have never considered myself as a man without a country. I'm very much an American and I deeply regret my inability to make films on American subjects, because they're the ones that interest me most.'

'But you're so at home here and in England.'

'True.' He ruminated for a moment and breathed heavily. 'I suppose America is really the bastard child of Britain. It certainly was at the beginning.'

★

'When I first appeared in Hollywood, I was the talk of the town and the moguls wanted to have a look at me as if to acquire me for their private zoo.

'One evening I was at a private dinner with all the major players of the time, Jack Warner, Sam Goldwyn and so on. After dinner, the wives and girlfriends politely withdrew into another room and we men were left at the table for cognac and cigars. They stared at me to regale them with witty stories from New York. After all, I was the new kid on the block. So, I tried and began to tell a long and elaborate story. Don't forget I was about forty years younger than all these guys and they were monsters, monsters, and they were all looking at me like a group of voracious dinosaurs.

'As I approached the end of the story, I realised I had forgotten the punchline.

'I was in trouble. Big trouble.

'So I prayed as never before in my life. I prayed for God to help me and in return I would give him anything He might want in the future.

'As the final moment arrived and I still hadn't remembered the payoff joke to my tale, I was sweating profusely, but still had my audience in the palm of my hand.

'Then something extraordinary happened. There was an earthquake, quite substantial, which shook the house, and the chandelier above the table crashed down. Glass and silverware on the table exploded everywhere and we all fled from the room.

'I was saved!'

I often thought about that story. It was as if Mr Welles had made a Faustian pact with the Devil. Maybe the Devil got his payback, not in one big payment but in dribs and drabs through the years as the glittering young man was slowly brought down, humiliated and rejected by the controlling powers of cinema, until he finally gave out just a few yards from where they lived in their mighty mansions.

'Ask not what you can do for your country. Ask what's for lunch.'

5

Catch-22 – The Aftermath

Citizen Kane was run on a Saturday evening after yet another day of muscular Christianity. That black and white, melodramatically angled and performed piece of pure American baroque awed, confused and impressed me.

I still marvel at the fact that when I first met Mr Welles he had already written, directed and starred in a film that predicted himself in later life humiliatingly trying to promote a not very gifted actress. Charles Foster Kane, William Randolph Hearst and George Orson Welles: how weak is man?

Talk about life following art – or was Mr Welles simply a clairvoyant?

★

'Rosebud is a dollar book Freudian gag which doesn't work. It's the thing I like least about Kane.'

★

Who was this Orson Welles who had not only written and directed it, but also starred in it? And hadn't he been aged only 24 when he pulled off this tour de force? The effect of the film, with its immaculate balance of intrigue, entertainment, mystery and drama, was immediate, and at once seduced me.

'It's Orson Welles,' said my father casually, as he handed me the phone.

'Hello, Mr Welles,' I said, as I put the receiver to my ear.

'When are you coming back to London?' the inimitable voice said.

'Tomorrow,' I replied.

'Come and see me,' Mr Welles commanded, and the phone went dead.

That habit of ending phone calls abruptly, I was, in future days, to grow used to. Once the reason for the phone call had been achieved, it was ended. No goodbyes.

'Well,' said my father, 'Do you think he'll offer you a job?' Back to the same old cry from the war generation, that somehow a job was security for ever.

'I hope so,' I answered. Because I did hope he would.

I had just spent a couple of days with my father and stepmother in Geneva, where they lived, telling them about my adventure. It was ironic that it had taken place in Yugoslavia where, the previous summer, we had returned for a few days on holiday. The journey had been filled with emotion, since it was the first time my stepmother, Katerina Dragalioup Stojesiljevic, had returned to her homeland since 1939 when she left Belgrade on the eve of hostilities, as the young bride of the Yugoslav Military Attaché to the Royal Court of Romania in Bucharest. It was her second marriage, as she was the widow of her first love, who had died of influenza at the age of 23.

The following year, Nazi Germany occupied oil-rich Romania and invaded Yugoslavia. She was forced to flee via the Black Sea and ended up in Egypt teaching Serbo-Croat to young British operatives who were being parachuted into Yugoslavia, either to support the Chetniks under Draža Mihailović, who were Serb royalists, or the partisans under the ruthless Tito. Her brother Nikola, my uncle by marriage and a young cavalry officer, cast in his lot with Mihailović and was rewarded for his patriotic efforts by two years' imprisonment at the end of the war. He never spoke to me about the war years, but the sadness in his eyes told me a lot. Like many citizens of oppressed or invaded nations, he calmly accepted what little life gave him without complaint or question.

My stepmother didn't like the idea of Miss Palinkaš being a Croat, but she was a fan of Orson Welles, having spent two years in Hollywood as a clothes designer just after the war ended. Welles must have been close to his peak at that time, with *Citizen Kane* under his belt, Rita Hayworth as his wife and who knows what glories ahead.

★

'Hello, boy,' said Mr Welles, without getting out of the deep sofa he was wedged in. We were in Ann Rogers' comfortable Maida Vale flat. 'Do you want to work for me?' he asked.

'Very much,' I replied.

'I'm going to send you to Rome to learn to cut. If you want to be a director, you need to learn to edit first. You can learn with Renzo Lucidi while I am in Mexico making *Catch-22* with Mike Nichols. Mrs Rogers will make the arrangements and I'll be back in Europe in a few weeks. I'll see you tomorrow.'

With that, I was summarily dismissed.

The next morning, I met Mrs Rogers at her house and we went in a chauffeur-driven Rolls-Royce to pick up Mr Welles at his house in Knightsbridge – one of his perks while contracted as an actor, I was later to discover. (In the intervening times, we were to use a much more modest form of transport – my car.)

We swept out to Heathrow Airport and through into the first-class lounge of British Airways. Standing there was Charles Feldman with his wife, who was also travelling to Los Angeles. Mr Welles immediately attacked him verbally. 'That edit you ended up with was incomprehensible. Your editor, what's his name, was arguing with me on the set about how shots were going to cut together. He didn't know a damn thing about what he was doing.'

'I'm happy with it.'

'I'm sure you are. You don't know anything about how to cut film.'

'Well, that's how it ended up.' Feldman was clearly trying to take the tension out of the air, but Mr Welles was irked.

'The production was a shambles. That Sellers is a monster.'

'Well, he's a big star. I built the movie around him. By the way, it was he who suggested you as Le Chiffre.'

'So I have to thank him for that? He made all of our lives a misery. Late on set and refusing to shoot with me.'

'You hurt his feelings.'

Mr Welles now roared. 'I hurt his feelings? He just got miffed when Princess Margaret turned up and completely ignored him to talk to me! He's got an ego the size of London!'

'Who's talking, Orson? Come on!'

'You should have let me direct the picture! You had enough directors to make a football team!'

'True. Maybe I should have asked you.'

Mr Welles muttered more and turned away, while Feldman and his wife moved to a far corner of the lounge.

Later that year, Mr Welles told me he was in a lift with the equally large Wolf Mankowitz, the writer on the screenplay. As the lift doors opened, Peter Sellers rushed to get into the lift. Seeing the two men, he rushed away. 'I turned to Wolf and asked "How much does he weigh, for God's sake?"'

Whatever Mr Welles thought of Charles Feldman, they had produced *Macbeth* together on a rock-bottom budget from Republic Pictures and Feldman had gone on to make *The Glass Menagerie* and *A Streetcar Named Desire*.

The profligate production of the shambolic *Casino Royale* was almost as legendary as the subsequent Coppola production, *Apocalypse Now*. The only difference was that the latter became a halfway decent film. *Casino Royale* was Ian Fleming's first James Bond book and was brilliant. Hollywood, of course, thought better, and decided to spoof it up for some unaccountable reason. When a writer creates a series of books in a particular order, why not follow his plan rather than attempt to improve on what is successful?

They did it again with the wonderful Patrick O'Brian series about naval warfare in the time of Nelson. Instead of making a movie of the first book, they combined this, for some extraordinary reason, with the twelfth book in the series, a pointless exercise when they had their dream sitting in front of them, a franchise. What do they say? A camel is a horse designed by a group of Hollywood moguls.

Mr Welles, sadly, never was given an adequate budget, let alone a profligate one. In film-making, this is an almost impossible hurdle to get over.

With Mr Welles away in Mexico in Guaymas playing the ludicrous Brigadier General Dreedle, I only had fleeting news of the filming.

The arrival of Mr Welles, for two weeks of shooting in February, was just the therapy the company needed: at the very least, it gave everyone something to talk about. The situation was almost melodramatically ironic. Mr Welles, the great American director now unable to obtain big-money backing for his films, was being directed by 37-year-old Mike Nichols. And Mr Welles had tried, unsuccessfully, to buy *Catch-22* for himself in 1962, and was appearing in it to pay for *The Deep*.

The cast apparently spent days preparing for his arrival. *Touch of Evil* was flown in and microscopically reviewed. *Citizen Kane* was discussed over dinner. Tony Perkins, who had appeared in Welles's film, *The Trial*, was repeatedly asked What Orson Welles Was Really Like.

Nichols began to combat his panic by imagining what it would be like to direct a man of Welles's stature. He said: 'Before he came, I had two fantasies. The first was that he would say his first line, and I would say, "No, no, no, Orson!" Then I thought, perhaps not. The second was that he would arrive on the set and I would say, "Mr Welles, now if you'd be so kind as to move over here …" And he'd look at me, raise one eyebrow, and say, "Over there?"

And I'd say, "What? Oh, uh, where do you think it should be?"' Mr Welles told me he landed in Guaymas with Peter Bogdanovich, who was interviewing him for a Truffaut-Hitchcock type book. For the eight days it took to shoot his two scenes, he dominated the set.

'It wasn't difficult. They seemed mesmerised by me like some European dignitary. I just stood on the runway there telling them stories about how we make movies in Europe, dubbing in Bavaria, looping in Italy and shooting in Yugoslavia. They said I told Nichols how to direct and the crew where to put the camera. Nonsense. Just a myth. They even said I spent time telling Martin Balsam how to deliver a line. Mike Nichols managed to glide through the two-week shoot very smoothly. He is smooth. And clever. Funnily enough my role as General Dreedle worked for me and the rest of the cast who were nervous of me as they would be of a general.'

★

Mike Nichols struggled in his dealings with Mr Welles: 'What I wanted to say to Welles was this – I wanted to say, "I know you're Orson Welles, and I know I'm me. I never said I was Mike Nichols. Those other people said that." What I mean by that is that he's a great man. I know he's a great man. I never said I was. And of course, you can't say such things.

'We were talking about Jean Renoir one day on the set, and Orson said, very touchingly, that Renoir was a great man but that, unfortunately, Renoir didn't like his pictures. And then he said, "Of course, if I were Renoir, I wouldn't like my pictures either." And I wanted to say to him, "If I were Orson Welles, I wouldn't like my pictures either, and it's OK, and I agree with you, and what can I do?"'

★

One day, shortly after Mr Welles returned from Mexico, I took a call from Mike Nichols. He wanted to thank Mr Welles for his work and asked me to tell him he had called. I told him I was his new assistant and he began to talk openly to me:

'I was very moved by Orson. I knew what it felt like to be him in that situation, I am an actor, to come into a company in the middle, to have a tremendous reputation not to like acting, to be used to being in control, and I was sorry when people didn't see what that felt like. Where the camera is and what it does is so much a part of his life, it's … instinctive. How is he suddenly supposed to ignore it?

'Take somebody like Elizabeth Taylor, when she is acting, she knows where the light is and how close the shot is. Orson knows whether he's in focus or not. Literally. If you know that much, what are you supposed to do with it? You can't throw it away. And I know that if I were acting in a movie, it would be very hard for me not to say, "I wonder if you would be kind enough to consider putting the camera a little more there so that when I do this … ?" How do you kill that knowledge?'

'You know Nichols was obsessed with what he calls The Fall. The Beatles call it that. His films make money, big money. He has the Midas touch and he hates it. He almost can't wait for The Fall to come: when he makes a movie that fails financially he will be treated as mortal.

'Mine came many moons ago and I've learnt to live with it!'

'Because I'm somewhat upset by the Midas thing and also by the reaction to the Midas thing. I don't like a critic to tell me that I set out to make a success, because it's not true. There's enough worry in thinking that you set out to do the very best you could and came out with only a success – that's depressing about oneself. You know, none of the great movies has been a popular success. I can't think of any exceptions. But you accept that there's a great difference between yourself and the artists who make films. It's like when you're

14 years old and you realise that Tchaikovsky would have liked to be Mozart – he just didn't have a choice. And I'm not even making a comparison there. But you have to go on as yourself. I'd like to be better, but I can't.'

Johnnie Jordan, the leading aerial cameraman of the time, was killed on *Catch-22*. A year earlier, he had been filming the mass helicopter battle sequence in Japan for the Bond film *You Only Live Twice*. Suspended in a harness from one helicopter, his lower leg was cut off by the blades of another. Then, while in Mexico, he was setting up a shot from inside a B-25 Mitchell bomber when he fell clean through the bomb doors to his death. He hadn't been wearing a safety harness since it impeded him with his one leg.

I have often thought film crews have affinities to the military. After all, they 'shoot' film and 'reload' their cameras. Like Special Forces, they often 'push the envelope' and Jordan was certainly one of those: fearless, always trying to push the boundaries.

Another cameraman, a friend of mine, was making a documentary about the Paras in the Gulf. Trying to get a better camera position for a shot of them jumping, he fell out of the aeroplane. It was only after several long seconds that he remembered he was wearing a parachute. Once he was on the ground, the director asked him what the hell he was doing there.

6

The Trial

Oja returned for a while to Zagreb, her home, where Mr Welles had met her a few years earlier while making his film of Franz Kafka's *The Trial* with Anthony Perkins, later to become a good friend. Perkins was perfectly cast as K. He, and he alone, had that remarkable ability to project the helplessness and desolation within.

That Gothic masterpiece on totalitarianism haunts me to this day, with its unrelenting mood of helplessness and suppression. The scene of K's workplace, set in that cavernous space (an empty exhibition centre) filled with hundreds of desks where hundreds of secretaries sit typing like metronomes, is electrifying. The Albinoni music merely adds to the morose atmosphere.

★

'The Salkinds came to see me one day. I was on holiday with my wife and daughter in Austria. They turned up in a taxi which they didn't have the money to pay for, so I gave it to them. They wanted me to make Taras Bulba, *a great story. I told them they were already shooting it with Yul Brynner in Argentina. They seemed surprised, then pulled out a great list of titles.*

'"We want you to shoot one of these for us. Choose. Any one."

'My eyes drifted down the list, and just when it was running out I saw The Trial. *I loved the book and was a great fan of Kafka. Great atmosphere writer. He foresaw the totalitarian states of the 1930s.*

'"I'll do that," I said. They seemed pleased and went off. I don't think they even had the rights on the book! Anyway, that's how I got to direct the movie.'

'So they were gamblers?'

'I'd call them adventurers. There are few of them about. I admire bravery of any form in a man. It's what takes us beyond the norm. I think it's the greatest quality in any human being. It's what makes us immortal, it makes us gods.'

Silence fell as I digested his profundities.

★

'I thought the Albinoni adagio fitted brilliantly the mood of the film.'

'Yes, and I used some Gesualdo.'

'Gesualdo?'

'Yes. And that's a story. He was a Neapolitan prince, the Prince of Venosa. A Renaissance composer. His music would have been perfect for *The Duchess of Malfi*. It is sacred music, but I detect an air of menace about it. He was a murderer. A brutal murderer. He found his wife in bed with her lover and killed them both and mutilated their bodies in a grisly fashion. Horrific.'

A few weeks later, I had flashbacks of this imagery when I heard about the brutal slaying of Sharon Tate.

It was when living in Moscow some years later that I realised how brilliantly Kafka and Mr Welles had evoked those decades of oppression. I was to be constantly reminded of such imagery, where architecture and buildings dominate man by their sheer size and sense of foreboding.

★

There is a hotel in Moscow which was built during Stalin's halcyon days. Since it was to be placed opposite the Kremlin, Stalin himself was asked to agree the design. In the drawings, the architects pre-

sented an option of two facias on the front of the building. Stalin strode into the room, agreed the plan and walked out. Nobody dared ask him to choose option one or two for the choice of facia. They were too frightened.

So the hotel was built with the two facias, one on either side of the main entrance.

It is compounded by the story of the Georgian former seminarian's death. His staff were simply too scared to approach his body for a number of hours, thinking him to be still asleep and fearing his reaction if they woke him up.

That is my definition of terror. Apart, of course, from Wallenstein and the cats.*

---

* Albrecht von Wallenstein was one of history's most sinister characters. Schiller wrote a trilogy about him. Cruel, ruthless and driven by blind ambition, he commanded the Catholic armies during the Thirty Years War. As he approached with his soldiers, townsfolk would flee fearing his terrible retribution. Men, women and children could not escape his vengeance, and even domestic animals were put to the sword.

7

Across the Iron Curtain

I began to make plans for my journey to Rome and decided to drive down in my white Austin Mini.

There was a young American named Steve Shane whom I had met the previous summer in Geneva while working on a student film, made with no money, whose only claim to fame is that the second assistant cameraman was Howard Atherton, later a distinguished director of photography on such pictures as *Fatal Attraction*. When I was back in London in the autumn, I saw Steve a number of times and he even invited me to the theatre once, along with his elderly father who was visiting from Los Angeles. We saw a superb production of Brecht's *Galileo*.

Steve was keen to travel into Europe again and, to share costs, I asked him to come with me in my Mini. In early January 1969, we set off through Belgium into Germany. President Richard Nixon had just been inaugurated and Jan Palach had burnt himself to death in protest at the Soviet invasion of Czechoslovakia. As we drove down the autobahns of Germany, we discussed the situation. I was angry about it. In Frankfurt we applied at the Czech consulate for entry visas and extraordinarily were granted them. From there, we drove on to Munich where Mr Welles had asked me to go to take some publicity photographs of a series of statuettes sculpted by Oja.

Outside Munich we stayed at the charming old Bavarian hotel called the Hotel Grunwald, with its burly antique furniture,

hugely powerful central heating and views south over the Issar
River and the Bavarian Alps. The statuettes had been stored there
and I photographed them. Once this work was done, we had time
to go to Prague since I didn't need to be in Rome till the end of
the week.

Prague is so trendy now, it's difficult to remember that it had
really been a closed city since its liberation in 1945 by the Red
Army. During the ensuing twenty years, it had fallen under a veil
of Communist secrecy and totalitarian pollution from the foul
emissions of their factories.

We drove in thick snow towards the Iron Curtain border, which
lay just beyond the medieval city of Regensburg. It was snowing hard as we drove through a forest, past the last of the West
German border posts. Ahead lay the Iron Curtain. It was as if we
were actors in a John Le Carré movie.

Ahead in the distance, along the snow-covered road, I could
see the bright lights of the Communist border post. A fur-hatted
guard leapt out of the trees and waved us down, peered inside
my little car and waved us on. We passed a giant watch tower
standing on its stilted legs and emerged into the brutally illuminated border post. Czech guards swarmed around our car and
demanded our papers. In hindsight, the notion of a young Brit
and a young American crossing into Czechoslovakia a few weeks
after the country had been invaded by Communist Russia seems
like madness. I suppose it was.

The scene was reminiscent of so many films of the time like
The Ipcress File – snow falling on an already snow-covered road,
pine trees towering menacingly, powerful spotlights lighting
up the snow like day, and humourless border guards dressed in
greatcoats and fur caps carrying AK-47s. We were asked the usual
questions like where were we going, why were we visiting and
how long were we staying. But they didn't seem to think we were
suspicious and waved us through.

We drove across a moonlit Bohemia looking exactly as
one imagined it should, drank an excellent pilsen in a dingy

bar in Pilsen and headed for the ancient capital of Bohemia. Prague was a dark, baroque city, black with pollution. It was Kafkaesque with a faux Disneyesque skyline as I drove my car along the cobbled tramlined streets. One of the upsides to Eastern Europe, even to this day, is that the Communists never got round to improving the roads and buildings so, by and large, pre-war and even pre-First World War buildings tend to have survived.

This part of *Mittel Europ* seemed to specialise in thirty-year events. By 1968, Prague had been suppressed for the thirty years since the Nazis had marched into the Sudetenland. This was exactly the same length of time as the religious wars that scarred the country in the seventeenth century, only this time it was National Socialists versus Communists, rather than Catholics versus Protestants. And infinitely more brutal.

Costa-Gavras' *L'Aveu* (*The Confession*), which came out a couple of years later, wonderfully demonstrated the terror imposed on that poor country. The beaten-dog-faced Yves Montand, that wonderful discovery of Edith Piaf, perfectly mirrored the mournful Slovak, Alexander Dubček.

The theatrically evil-looking *Reichsprotecktor* of Bohemia, Reinhard Heydrich, as hideous as a great white shark in his immaculate Hugo Boss-manufactured SS uniform, was probably only just surpassed in nihilistic brutality by the shabby-suited Antonín Novotný and his henchmen, as Stalin tightened his grip on Czechoslovakia a decade after Hugo Boss materials, entangled in the explosive assassin's bullet, had entered Heydrich's bloodstream and poisoned him to death.

And now this thirty-year suppression imposed by Germans, and then Russians, was about to get worse. Alexander Dubček tried tentatively to soften the hand of government. He was warned by the Politburo to desist, but he didn't listen.

On 20 August, Czechoslovakia was invaded by the armies of her erstwhile allies, the Warsaw Pact, led by the iron fist of Mother Russia. No velvet glove here. I had been enjoying a latter-day

Habsburg holiday in Rijeka, visiting the haunts of the histrionic and quite implausible Gabriele D'Annunzio, when the mournful Slovak Dubček had been whisked away to Moscow, where he was subjected to the brutal bullying of Brezhnev in the Great Hall of the Kremlin. He was obliged to walk the full length of the enormous space to approach the Russian leader, each step emphasising his subservience to the Russian masters.

All this led to his removal from power, and the invasion of Czechoslovakia by the Red Army tanks manned by Kazaks and Uzbeks, who spoke no known European language and reacted with brutish bewilderment to the sophisticated taunting of the Czech students who stood in their way. They were hardly impressed by Jan Palach's self-immolation in protest against their presence, and certainly would have missed its significance in shadowing those other acts of self-immolation by anti-war Buddhist monks in Vietnam earlier that year.

★

When I told Mr Welles of my visit to occupied Prague, we lightened the mood by discussing that almost onomatopoeic word 'defenestration.' We decided it would be an excellent title for a movie, 'Defenestrator – the Ultimate Weapon.'

We wondered whether you could be 're-fenestrated,' but thought not. In any event, it's a modus operandi seemingly unique to Bohemia, with one defenestration in the late Middle Ages and the second during the Thirty Years War. It had a sinister epilogue when Jan Masaryk, the Czech national hero and foreign minister, was thrown to his death by Communist thugs in 1948.

Mr Welles chuckled about the Communist announcement that Masaryk had committed suicide by quoting the Czech reaction, 'Mr Masaryk was a very tidy man. He was so tidy that when he jumped from his bathroom, he closed the window.'

★

So, into Prague we drove and up into Wenceslas Square, which, by the way, is not a square at all but more of an avenue leading up to an enormous neo-baroque building, the National Museum.

We stayed in a modest hotel, sharing a vast room with a hand basin in the corner, and went out for a drink. Wandering along the darkened streets, we ducked into a bar. In the years that have passed since that time, I've often wondered about this coincidence. We ordered drinks and sat at the bar. At once a gentleman sitting to my right began to join in the conversation, asking where were we from, and so on. As the talk went on, I looked around me and noticed that there were no women about in this full bar. I realised that it was a gay bar and whispered this to Steve, saying we should leave. Outside, I made the usual jokes about of all the places in the entire world. And Steve laughed with me.

The next day, we visited the bullet-marked National Museum. When I say bullets, they were of considerably bigger calibre. They were the violent pockmarks of heavy machine-gun fire, big scars the size of a human fist, all over the sandy-coloured stucco of the ornate building. Inside the stiflingly dull and deserted museum, the only things that interested me were more of these machine-gun scars in the ceilings which had smashed the delicate frieze work. Rarely have I been in such a hugely uninteresting museum in such a hugely pretentious building, which I suppose you would call Central European Victorian bourgeois architecture. It posessed nothing of the magic of Prague Old Town with its Gothic spires and Bohemian rooftops.

Coming out of the museum, we noticed what looked like a bombsite in the street. There was a row of houses with a gaping hole in the middle. Since there are no earthquakes, to my knowledge, in Czechoslovakia, we investigated further. A bystander pulling on a cheap cigarette told us with a shrug that this had been the site of the Prague radio station and a Russian tank had reversed into it, letting the whole building collapse on top of it. The tank then drove off with the rubble cascading off it, their objective achieved – no radio station broadcasting anti-Soviet news.

I had heard of these sorts of tactics in Vietnam where, in a suspect village, the head man's house would be razed to the ground. After all, it was only a year after the Tet Offensive and the Battle of Hué, symbolised by those memorable Don McCullin pictures of exhausted US Marines, which still were etched on my mind.

Then came another reflection of Vietnam when, in Wenceslas Square, which is really the top of the boulevard leading up a slight hill to the National Museum, underneath the statue of Saint Wenceslas we came across a small area between all the traffic covered in flowers, many of which had been recently left there. Pretty soon we realised it was the site where, on 19 January, just a few days before I had arrived in Prague, Jan Palach, the young student, had burnt himself to death in protest against the Russian invasion. He was 21, three years younger than me, and he had had the raw courage to self-immolate himself as a sacrifice for his people. I envied him his raw courage and burning patriotism.

We English have not had that awful experience of our country being crushed under the heel of alien jackboots. In photographs, I saw the face of a determined and handsome young patriot, perhaps mindful of the 1415 burning of the great Czech religious reformer, Jan Hus. It seems the peoples of Central Europe have so often in history been crushed, either by barbarians from the East or dictatorships from the West. They do not have the good fortune of that narrow strip of water – the English Channel – which has so often down the centuries protected us from those who would do us harm.

Later that day, we were walking in another part of the city where I photographed a street sign saying '*Namesti Jana Palacha*' (Jan Palach Square). This square had previously been known as the Square of the Red Army. This had been painted out and repainted by the municipal painter in honour of Palach. To my knowledge, this sign was only up for a short period of time before the authorities repainted it. I still have the photograph.

We wandered into the Old Town Square, with its Gothic pointed towers, and along the little street where we found Franz Kafka's birthplace. It was all dark and black with soot, not the painted cake it is these days.

We left Prague by the north-west road and visited the site of the village of Lidice, which had been targeted by the Nazis on 10 June 1942 in reprisal for the assassination of Reinhard Heydrich, the deputy *Reichsprotecktor* of Bohemia and Moravia. We stood below the giant memorial to the decimated village that had been laid waste by the Nazis. The snow-covered hills and the low grey sky reflected the sombre mood of Eastern Europe perfectly.

The Germans had targeted the village shortly after the sinister Heydrich had died of his wounds on 4 June. They had been inflicted by the Czech Resistance fighters, Jan Kubiš and Jozef Gabčík, a week before in an attack on his car as he drove to work in Prague. The Germans shot most of the men and boys up against the walls of a local farm and deported the women and children, either to concentration camps or, if the children were ethnically German, to suitable educational institutes. In all, more than 300 people were killed.

In January of that year, Heydrich had been one of the chief architects of the Holocaust at the so-called Wannsee Conference. Now he was dead, deemed a hero by Hitler, and in particular Himmler.

As we rejoined the main road we watched as a Soviet armoured division lumbered past, belching out black fumes from their exhausts. Once brutally occupied by Nazi Germans, they were now brutally occupied by Communist Russians. When would all this end? The sad face of Dubček seemed to reflect the nature of their fate.

That afternoon we drove on to Karlovy Vary, or Carlsbad, where Beethoven, Brahms, Wagner and Tolstoy had taken the waters. We took tea in the massive and depressing Hotel Moskva, formerly the magnificent Grandhotel Pupp where, in the nineteenth century, the grandees of Central Europe had taken time off to forget their satanic mills and dark factories manned by restless employees. Karl Marx had also taken the waters here.

A young waiter with a frayed collar and stained waistcoat served us. He tried his halting English with us, not daring to ask what on earth we were doing in a recently reoccupied Communist country deep in Eastern Europe.

'Where is Dubček now?' I asked.

He shrugged his shoulders and smiled uneasily. 'Who knows? For a little time he gave us hope.' Then he hurried away past the faded sofas and the gilt mirrors which had probably reflected Austro-Hungarian princes, wealthy Jewish merchants from Vienna, and grey-coated Nazi officers during the war, followed by drearily clad and unhealthy bureaucrats from East Germany and Poland, with their fat opulent wives watching disapprovingly as their inattentive husbands ogled the fresh-faced young Bohemian girls and boys who served them.

As the sun began to fade, we re-crossed the German border and headed towards Munich once again. I mentioned these thoughts to Steve and he agreed with my imagery.

'It must have been the only way out of what was hell,' said Steve.

'What?' I replied, peering into the snow-covered road ahead.

'Sex,' he said.

'Oh, you mean selling yourself for money? For a pretty girl, yes.'

'And for an attractive boy as well.'

'Why not?' I mumbled.

Many years later, when living in Hong Kong, I was filming in Los Angeles and, on a whim, looked up the name Shane in the telephone book. There were only a few Shanes in the book, and after three failures I dialled once more. As the phone rang interminably, I whispered, 'Shane! Shane!' in a high-pitched voice like Brandon deWilde at the end of George Stevens' brilliant movie. I knew the boy actor's name because he had been killed the year before in a car accident in Denver and he will forever be remembered for his performance in that movie. The crunch of Jack Palance's boots on the duckboards outside the town bar haunt me even to this day.

An old man's voice answered. I instantly lowered my voice tone from alto to tenor and asked to speak to Steve.

'He's dead,' came the abrupt reply.

'Oh, I'm sorry,' I lamely replied.

Silence hung along the static on the telephone wires.

'Is that Mr Shane, Steve's father?' I persisted.

'Yes,' came another abrupt reply.

'Do you remember me? I was a friend of Steve's in London. Dorian Bond. You took us to a play at the Mermaid Theatre – *Hadrian the Seventh* starring Alec McCowan, do you remember?'

I could now hear thinking on the line.

'No,' the voice said.

There was another lengthy pause before I heard another voice, the phone obviously grabbed. And it went dead. All I had was the dialling tone.

'Sod this,' I thought to myself and dialled again.

This time it was the voice of an old lady, presumably Mrs Shane.

'I'm sorry to bother you, Mrs Shane, but I wanted to contact you since I was a friend of Steve in London.'

'I understand,' she said. 'I apologise, my husband is losing it a little. I have to tell you that sadly our son, Steven, killed himself up in San Francisco three years ago. He was such a sweet boy. He died in what was apparently the deliberate crash of a glider. We know because he dictated a last message into a tape machine which he left in his car at the airfield. He said he couldn't live with the fact that he was homosexual.'

Silence fell.

'I'm so sorry,' I whispered. 'He was such a nice chap. I had no idea. We did a lot together. We drove back from Geneva to London in his clapped-out old Citroen 2CV at the end of that summer. It rained most of the journey and the windscreen wipers didn't work so I had to spend most of my time with my arm reaching out of the horizontal flap of the window with the broken wiper in my hand to clear the windscreen.'

'That must have been fun for you!' Mrs Shane laughed, 'You must come round for a cup of tea with us. We are old now, but it would be darling to meet you. You should also meet Steven's sister, Celeste, she is very beautiful. Are you married, Mr Bond?' Even though she had never met me, Mrs Shane, like so many Americans before and since, was evidently enchanted by my English accent. There's many a deadbeat Englishman who has traded on his clipped pronunciation to advance himself in the old colonies.

The following day, I turned up in the gravel drive of an enormous mock-Tudor mansion overlooking Hollywood. If it wasn't Pickfair, it looked darned like it. I felt as if I was in suburban Surrey in the 1930s. I could even hear the sounds of people playing tennis. After ringing the doorbell I had to wait for a good long time until I heard shuffling behind the door. Clearly it was the maid's day off.

A more dishevelled and elderly Mr Shane than I remembered in London opened the door after much unlocking and unbolting. Remember, this wasn't that long after the Manson family killings, so people living in vast mansions in the Hollywood hills felt vulnerable. Charles Manson had single-handedly destroyed the notion of flower power. Hippies were no longer the innocent bearers of love and kindness, because maybe behind the long hair and beads they had another agenda.

As Mr Shane slowly opened the door, his glamorously coiffured elderly wife came forward and greeted me. 'Hello, you're the young man who worked for Orson Welles, aren't you? We saw a very young Orson Welles play Tybalt in a wonderful production of *Romeo and Juliet* at the Mainstreet Theatre, as it was known then. Katharine Cornell played Juliet. She must have been already 40 by then, but she was a most beautiful and sensitive Juliet. I think she was probably America's greatest actress. Don't you agree, honey?'

Mr Shane stared at her, thinking back. 'Maybe. All I know she was very attractive. Shame she was a lesbian.'

'Really, honey, can you not use such language.'

'And she was married to a faggot,' he persisted, laughing.

'Guthrie McClintic was, I'll have you know, a great theatre producer.'

As a child of the '60s, I had never heard of these legendary theatrical figures until Mr Welles told me about them.

Mrs Shane turned away from her husband, who had suddenly come to life, 'Steven always talked about you. He was very fond of you.'

'I'm so sorry that this has happened,' I mumbled inadequately.

Steve had told me about his parents. He was an afterthought, probably a mistake, and they were more like grandparents to him than parents. His father had made a fortune selling cars in Kansas City just after the war. America was booming and he was coining it. He then acquired the Rolls-Royce and Bentley franchise for southern California and moved to Beverly Hills. What better place to sell a Rolls, I thought to myself.

It was an embarrassing meeting since, clearly, the two parents thought I had been one of their son's boyfriends. Mrs Shane then rang her daughter, Celeste, whom Steve had often talked about, and told her I was in town and that maybe she should introduce me to Anjelica. Celeste, known always as 'Cici,' was married at that time to the ageing John Huston. And the then-unknown Anjelica Huston had just started her long and tempestuous relationship with Jack Nicholson. Clearly, I was on the bench for what seemed to be the Major Leagues. Or I thought I was. (I should explain that Cici was a close friend of Anjelica Huston as they had been almost exact contemporaries in Los Angeles.) Cici, whom of course I never met, politely declined her mother's suggestion.

After we had discussed the performance of *Hadrian the Seventh* that Mr Shane had taken Steve and me to in London, about which he had absolutely no recall, the conversation dwindled. Clearly Mr Shane thought I was making it all up and was some sort of fraud. Mrs Shane, on the other hand, persistently tried to think of socialites I should meet.

I brought the conversation to an abrupt halt when I said that whenever I thought of Kansas, I thought of the Clutter family murders, of Truman Capote's extraordinary book on the subject and Richard Brooks' chilling black and white film with its Conrad Hall cinematography portraying that desolate Kansas skyline and Quincy Jones' harsh music background. I was on a roll of enthusiasm, as any former film student would be.

Silence fell.

'We don't like to think of Kansas like that. We like to think of Kansas more with *The Wizard of Oz*.' With that, Mrs Shane, ever the polite hostess, indicated that my visit was at an end and showed me to the door. I didn't have the heart to point out to them that the beginning of that movie, also in black and white, had also been somewhat menacing. As I shook Mr Shane's hand, he stared at me suspiciously, still convinced that he had never met me before in his life.

As I drove slowly down the winding road into Beverly Hills, I thought about that back of beyond, Kansas. I thought about how Truman Capote had read a report of the Clutter murders in the *New York Times* and, along with his childhood friend, Harper Lee, set off for Kansas to investigate. He felt that Harper Lee, who had just finished the manuscript of *To Kill a Mockingbird*, would be better able communicate with the locals. And the result had been that remarkable book, which, along with Vincent Bugliosi's *Helter Skelter*, still heads the all-time bestseller lists of non-fiction novels.

I had just bought the newly published *Helter Skelter* from a bookshop on Rodeo Drive and was immersed in it as it brought back memories of Mr Welles and Sharon Tate in Rome. I also recalled talking with Mr Welles and John Huston about Capote, who had written the script for Huston on *Beat the Devil*. Huston had told Mr Welles that the 5ft 3in high-pitched-voiced Capote had been terrified of meeting the giant Mr Welles, with his booming voice. He knew this because Capote had told him he had written to Tennessee Williams for his advice on how to deal with him.

Here I was heading up my own company, producing a series of highly priced TV commercials for Hong Kong in Los Angeles and yet somehow the distinctive giant shadow of Mr Welles was cast over me still. I comforted myself with the smug thought that my budget from an international tobacco company was more than Mr Welles had been given by Republic Pictures for his *Macbeth*. But that depressed me more. He had made *Macbeth*, and I was making a series of infinitely forgettable TV commercials. He was definitely on higher moral ground.

★

'When on tour around America, I used to play cards with the great Katharine Cornell on the afternoons we didn't have a matinee. One afternoon in Kansas City, for God's sake, we had this crazy idea of being clairvoyants. For some reason, she knew all their tricks. We charged the public to come in for readings but gave them back their money at the end of each session. I know all their expressions. It's an occupational disease of fortune-tellers. First you do the cold reading, where you state the obvious. Then you become a shut-eye.

'She was a very beautiful forty then, too old for Juliet, you might think. But not at all, with her distinctive elocution and her physicality, she portrayed all the passion and emotion that lies within that part. I was a callow youth of eighteen! Can you imagine?'

'You must have been cute,' laughed Oja.

'Dorian, have you ever heard of this woman?'

'Vaguely,' I answered.

'Vaguely?' he thundered, 'She was probably America's greatest theatre actress. America's answer to Sybil Thorndyke, Eleonora Duse and even Sarah Bernhardt. She and her husband produced great plays, successful plays, Candida *for Bernard Shaw and* The Barretts of Wimpole Street.

'They brought over many of England's leading actors to America and gave them their Broadway debuts – Larry Olivier, John Gielgud, Ralph Richardson. They gave me my Broadway break, for God's sake!'

Another baritone chuckle, before a quaff of red wine ...

8

The Eternal City

I said goodbye to Steve in Munich and headed on south in a snowstorm over the Bavarian and Austrian Alps into Italy via the Brenner Pass. I had to fix chains onto my tyres to ensure the car's grip on the slippery snow and, as I lay under the wheels fixing them, was glad of the sheepskin jacket I had purchased from a Palestinian shepherd in the hills outside Bethlehem the year before.

In the early morning, I visited the enormous Italian monument to their war dead of the First World War, near Trento, and thought of the young Hemingway and *For Whom the Bell Tolls*. Whenever people make light of Italian military prowess, I quote them this campaign, which might have gone forgotten, were it not for Hemingway, against the traumas of the Western Front. The joke about the book of Italian war heroes is inaccurate. My theory is that Italians, as individuals, are as heroic and brave as any nation in the world. But two or more Italians are a different matter. They discuss the pros and cons of impending violence, agree that everyone will be friends anyway within a very short period of time, and agree not to fight. That sounds like civilised and intelligent behaviour to me. It was the manager of the Hotel Piazza di Spagna, the grey-haired and sallow Andrea, who enlightened me on this. One evening, I asked him what he did in the war. He answered me brilliantly.

'*Era un grande casino! Prima Mussolini e Africa e Libya e poi sono stato in Albania e Grecia con l'Armia.*'*

Captain Corelli's Mandolin hadn't been written then and all I knew was there were some horrendous conditions in the snow of the Macedonian mountains and some idyllic conditions on the Greek islands, which had been occupied by the Italians many years before the war.

'We were in the army – *L'Armia d'Amore*, we called ourselves, and the Greek girls loved us,' Andrea sighed and raised his hands in supplication.

I had coffee in Verona, with a lightness in the air that intimated to me that I was south of the Alps and spring was not far away. Mr Welles was still away and I had a month to learn the art of editing in one of the most ancient cities in the world. I drove out of Verona, past its great Roman arena, and headed south. The flat plains of Lombardy lay ahead of me, with mist lying all across the marshy land which formed the flood basin of the mighty River Po.

The morning sun was breaking through the mist when suddenly, on the distant horizon, I saw towers, turrets, cupolas and domes and the battlements of a medieval city. It was Mantua, lying mysteriously among its limpid lagoons at the end of winter, mosquito free. I was driving towards the city across the Ponte Legnano – the long causeway that ran across the two mist-covered lakes that formed a gigantic moat protecting this strange place. Locals call it the 'sleeping beauty,' *La Bella Addormentata*, and it hasn't changed much since the high Middle Ages. The key to this is the lakes themselves, natural defences 1,000 years old that protected Mantua from the outside world.

The size of the city was pretty much what it had been in the time of La Gran Contessa (historical proof that the fairer sex is not the weaker sex), who had ruled the city with a fist of iron, not encumbered by a velvet glove, as the First Crusade had passed by its walls.

---

*   'It was a disaster! First Mussolini and Africa and Libya and then I was posted to Albania and Greece in the army.'

I parked in the deserted car park and walked across the cobbled Piazza Sordello to the Palazzo Ducale, the second largest palazzo in all of Italy after the Vatican. And Italy is a land of palazzos. The private palazzo of the Gonzaga family is straight from a blood-soaked early seventeenth-century English play – long, deserted, damp corridors full of menace; banqueting halls with Mantena frescoes fading fast on the damp walls; colonnades passing overgrown Renaissance gardens that had once witnessed whispered plots, vile assassinations and lustful assignations; strange miniature doorways for the duke's personal dwarfs. Altogether, it was a feast for the imagination, peopled by princes and cardinals from long ago, all ruled by the sinister Gonzaga family.

For 400 years, this had been the home of the Gonzaga family, the now extinct Dukes of Mantua, who had held sway here until 1707, putting their stamp on everything, much as the Medicis did in Florence. The labyrinth includes a castle, basilica, courtyards, sumptuous galleries, gardens and more than 500 rooms. Unfortunately, most of them are closed off, but there is still plenty to see, from precious tapestries, a glittering mirror gallery and masterpieces by Raphael, to a zodiac painted on a psychedelic sixteenth-century ceiling fresco by Lorenzo Costa.

I stumbled upon a couple of hidden jewels by the hotel, with scarcely a visitor in sight: the intimate eleventh-century Rotonda di San Lorenzo, inspired by Jerusalem's Holy Sepulchre Church, and the fabulous rococo Teatro Bibiena, where the 13-year-old Mozart once performed.

★

'I wanted to shoot Webster's Duchess of Malfi in that palazzo. It would have been marvellous. Webster would have been a great screenwriter. I tried to do Malfi on the London stage with Micheál Mac Liammóir but it didn't work out. I ended up directing Olivier in Ionesco's Rhinoceros. It was a disaster. Olivier would take direction then go round behind my back and do exactly what he wanted.

*I hated the whole experience. He humiliated me. By the way, I hated
the play anyway. The only thing was that poor old Ionesco had spe-
cially asked for it to be directed by me.'*

★

Springtime in Rome was sunny and warm and welcoming. Its
terracotta stucco and stone colours exuded the warmth of the
Mediterranean and I understood at once the blasé Lombardi attitude to their capital as being in the 'south.' Northern Italians draw
a line across their country just where Tuscany ends; beyond that
is what they consider the foreign 'south.'

After driving around for a while, up and down and around
cobblestoned streets festooned with brightly coloured washing
lines and not changed in width nor surface since the Renaissance,
I parked randomly up against a stucco wall. As I got out, a Vespa
rider hooted and buzzed past me. I wandered into the endlessly
fashionable Via Condotti, Rome's answer to Beverly Hills' Rodeo
Drive, and settled at a table of the Caffé Greco. I marvelled at
the eighteenth-century-style décor, not knowing at this point
that Goethe, Byron, Stendhal, Mendelssohn and Ibsen had taken
refreshments here. And, of course, it was just across the way
from the house where John Keats had expired from tuberculosis
at the age of 24. I wondered whether even he had had his coffee
here in the mornings.

Revitalised by an almost solid espresso, I meandered into the
sunny streets of a spring morning in Rome and chanced on a
modest *pensione* with the very original name of the Pensione Piazza
di Spagna, located as it was just behind the famous Spanish Steps.

I bought a *Teach Yourself Italian* book and attended Renzo
Lucidi's editing rooms the following morning. Lucidi was one
of Italy's most well-known film editors and an old friend of
Mr Welles. He had been his editor on the stunning *Othello* and
also on *Mr Arkadin* (known in the UK as *Confidential Report*),
and had edited a number of well-known Italian movies during
the early 1960s.

When I first got there, he immediately took me in his Alfa Romeo out to the fabled Cinecittà Studios, where he was the supervising editor on a spaghetti Western named *A Man Called Sledge*, starring James Garner and Dennis Weaver.

As he drove he talked. 'Orson is a crazy son of a bitch. *È completamente pazzo. Veramente matto.* When he sent me the material for *Othello*, it was a *cassinissimo*: different types of film stock developed in different laboratories and different countries and photographed by different cameramen. Thank God it was in black and white. In colour it would have been more of a disaster. Half of it was synchronised sound, half *sensa* sound. Some with *doppiagio*, some not.'

Renzo was quite carried away by this time, driving faster and faster, with a cigarette in one hand and the steering wheel in the other, interspersed with his elbow pressing on the horn whenever needed. Even by Rome's insane driving standards, this was crazy driving. 'I love him, I love him, but on *Othello* he had, I think, seven different Desdemonas. Seven!' He pronounced Desdemona vehemently on the second syllable rather than the third, so I couldn't grasp the word.

'Desdemona?' I checked.

'Yes, yes, yes, Desdemona,' he shrieked, again on the second syllable. 'One speak no English at all. With Shakespeare *impossibile*.'

'Who was that?'

'You don't know? My God, everybody in Italy knows! The beautiful Lea Padovani. She a good actress but *inutile* in English. Orson *inamorata di lei, inamorata*. Obsessed with her, he chase her from post to pillar all over Italy. He even pay for her to have English lessons. And she never sleep with him! Only one time *e basta*. One time is enough for her. She very small, he very big.'

'I know,' I answered.

'I have a cocktail next week in my apartment. You will meet Lea there. She very nice and her English much better now. But for Desdemona, *mai*. Orson, he crazy, but I love him.'

Renzo calmed down as we cleared the crowded streets of the ancient capital and headed for Cinecittà.

This was the golden age of spaghetti westerns, which started with the extraordinary success of *A Fistful of Dollars*, made in 1963 by Sergio Leone, a non-English-speaking Italian director of sand-and-sandals productions. Taking a Kurosawa samurai story, he shot the film mainly on location in Almeria, south-eastern Spain, to replicate a Mexican look. A TV series actor who had never made a big film was cast as the hero – Clint Eastwood, a 30-year-old actor who had starred in the TV series *Rawhide* but was now fading fast in popularity. A friend recommended him to Leone and he accepted an offer of $15,000 plus a free Mercedes on completion of a planned three-month shoot. He became a worldwide star and never looked back.

The film, with its Ennio Morricone (who had been at school with Leone) music track, made millions from its simplistic but dramatic visuals and next-to-no dialogue, making it very saleable in markets all over the world. Two more follow-ups were made. *For a Few Dollars More* and *The Good, the Bad and the Ugly* followed swiftly in the ensuing years and everybody jumped on the bandwagon. In the following decade, more than 600 of these European-based Westerns were produced.

A Man called Sledge was just another of these. When filming in Spain, I have often wondered whether the conquistadores settled in Mexico because it looked like a home away from home.

In this production, the producers had not cast an unknown actor. Having parked up behind the set, we walked through the sets of *Ben Hur*, down what was effectively a full-up western town. Here I was, within a few miles of the centre of Rome, walking down a street straight out of the wild west.

Lucidi walked on to the set, which had broken for a change of set-up and started talking to a very red-faced James Garner. He was a huge star, having just appeared in *The Great Escape*, *The Americanisation of Emily* and *Grand Prix* – big films of that time. Garner is the classic example of the truth that if you give actors bad scripts they look bad and if you give them good scripts they look good. Although he made *A Man Called Sledge* and a number of other bad films, he also later made the hugely successful *Rockford Files* and starred in the wonderful *Victor Victoria*, as well as *The Notebook* and *Space Cowboys*. His career was long and successful. He was one of the lucky ones, unlike myriads of other jobbing actors who take work as it comes along to make a living.

The notion that actors 'read screenplays' and like them is a myth. If Steven Spielberg sends you a script you just say 'yes' before reading anything because you know it's money and you have to pay the mortgage, or the school fees, or taxes, or whatever. The conversation with the agent goes along these lines:

'How do you feel about two weeks in the South of France?'

'Sounds good to me.'

'Working with Tom Cruise and Susan Sarandon.'

'Fantastic. When?'

'Tomorrow.'

'And the money?'

'Three hundred thousand plus first-class air fares for you and your wife and accommodation in a five star hotel, all expenses paid.'

'I'll take it.'

'Do you want me to send you the script?'

'F*** the script.'

Mr Welles did this many, many times in his life. He was a jobbing actor and had been since the age of 18.

Renzo taught me the basics of editing on the horizontal table editing machine, used in Europe at that time. (In the US and UK, movie editors, by and large, used the upright Moviola vertical spool system. During the more recent past, these systems have been superseded by computerised editing such as Avid.)

During the ensuing weeks, I continued to learn the mechanics of editing, watched the shooting of a spaghetti western starring James Garner shot at Cinecittà and edited by Renzo Lucidi, endlessly walked the narrow red streets of Rome, and spent hours in baroque Roman churches, ornate art galleries and elegant restaurant-filled piazzas.

Renzo told me stories of Mr Welles when he had first come to Italy just after the war:

'He was a mystery to us then. The war had only just finished and neo-realism was fashionable here. Orson was like a great bear from North America. Nobody had seen any of his films but we had heard about them. He hit Rome like a bomb. He flew himself out here with a British pilot and nearly crashed on the way. Then he stayed at the Excelsior on the Via Veneto, held political press conferences, announced a number of film projects, and chased women like a man obsessed. He even had a little affair with Jennifer Jones when she came out here to make *Stazione Termini* for Vittorio De Sica opposite Montgomery Clift. Her husband at the time, Selznick, became very *agitato* since Orson and she were seen out night after night in different restaurants. Maybe they were just good friends!'

'I think he has a thing for dark-haired women, the Latin look.'

'Yes, Dorian, you are right. In those days he was working on about three different projects, *Othello*, which he paid for from his own money and he still owes me more, that crazy *Caliostro* film where he dressed up like a gypsy and even *The Third Man*. All the money he made he put into *Othello* and we all went along with him. He is a natural film-maker, he is an artist. You are lucky to work with him. It is an honour.'

'It certainly is,' I replied.

'I bet he doesn't pay you properly?'

'No,' I shrugged, 'but who cares. Just being with him is enough.'

'*Exacto*, my friend. You will learn much from him, but in the end, you will have to leave him. Otherwise he will drag you down with him like the *Titanic*.'

The imagery unnerved me, but I soon forgot those prophetic words.

'Anyway, let's work more. Next week I am having a cocktail party I want you to come to. You can meet my friends. Lea is coming.'

'Padovani?'

'*Exacto*,' he smiled. 'You can ask her all about Orson.'

Lea Padovani gazed down at me from a glamorous black and white publicity shot of the fifties.

'He was crazy for her,' said Alessandro Tasca, 'crazy for her.'

I looked at the alluring woman who had captured the heart of Orson Welles just twenty years before in this self-same place.

Tasca shrugged his shoulders in that typically Italian gesture of hopelessness. 'There was nothing we could do. It drove him to insanity and she never recovered. She lived with him but she never slept with him. Except once and that was a disaster. He told me. And he always thought himself a consummate lover.'

'So what happened?'

'I don't know. No one will ever know.'

Eventually the summons came from Mr Welles via the loyal Ann Rogers, his sort of latter-day Miss Moneypenny. I was to go to Paris and meet him there at the LTC laboratories in St Cloud, where his material from the previous winter in Yugoslavia had been processed.

I flew up to Paris and hired a cutting room with its editing table and waited in the darkness for the big man. I heard him in the corridor before I saw him. His voice was big, like him, but tenor rather than bass and polished by his immaculate articulation, doubtless nurtured by his mother and Roger Hill, his school teacher, from whom he learnt his love of Shakespeare. As he walked in, I looked at him afresh having learnt so much about him from people who knew him in Rome. His reputation went before him.

★

The tiny, almost bird-like Lea Padovani had described him to me at the Lucidi party almost with regret in her strongly accented voice.

'*He was so enveloping, so wanting to consume me, like one of his gigantic meals. He never left me alone after I first was introduced to him. I was in love with someone else, but he completely disregarded that. He turned up in the audience of a play I was doing, Noel Coward actually, night after night. Then always he came to my dressing room after the show with a huge bunch of flowers. After a week I had so many my room was like a tropical jungle! He was magnificent, proud, and all he wanted to do was seduce me.*'

The same thought had occurred to me, as I listened to her. Ridiculous as it may seem – I was 24 and she 50 – she was still vibrantly attractive with Cleopatra eyes and a voluptuous mouth.

'*He got fatter and fatter like some monster and I really wasn't attracted to him physically. Mentally, yes, he was funny, witty, clever – everything you want in a man, except he did not appeal to me.*'

'*So why did you stay with him for so long?*'

'*So, you know something?*'

'*Only what Renzo has told me.*'

'*Once involved with Orson and his life it is like being in a spider's web. He is complex, cunning and always surprising. Life is never boring with him. I never had the courage to run away.*'

She turned away and took a long drag on her cigarette. I gulped down another swig of my Campari. 'And you, young man. You are young and beautiful. What are you doing with him?'

'*Just learning from him.*'

She pointed at me with a judgemental finger. 'Be careful. He is very intoxicating and you end up going nowhere.'

A very tanned and handsome middle-aged man approached her, whispered in her ear, and she laughed as she moved away on his arm. 'Gianni tells me I am la cigogne, *a baby-snatcher, talking to you!*'

Later that evening she called across to me as I said my goodbyes, 'And his feet are too small for his body.'

I walked out into the warm Roman night and thought about her random remark ...

★

His face, hands and feet were indeed altogether smaller and more delicate than the sheer bulk of his body, indicating a refined and civilised man at odds with his physical proportions. He was dressed in his usual black – black slacks with black lace-up shoes and socks, black loose-fitting shirts worn outside his slacks, black jacket or cloak depending on the weather. In his hand, a notebook and box of Havana cigars. He never wore a watch.

He spoke fluent Italian, French and Spanish. So, he was the quintessential Europeanised American, more so than Fitzgerald or Hemingway, and his films after *Touch of Evil* were all European. More of that later.

I'm sure the wives and women in his life could tell you much more in this intimate territory than I ever could, but I'm just telling you how it all seemed to me, in my Englishness at that time.

Mr Welles and I looked at the footage he had shot those months before, breathing heavily, cigar in hand. As he watched those images he began to talk to me, but really to himself, almost anonymously in the darkness: 'Mike Nichols was a nice man. A very nice man. He was patient with me. He comes out of that New York theatre world, like I did. Then he did that Virginia Woolf movie which I never saw, but I loved the stage play. Albee was a genius. It was never more than a play, never a film. After that he did *The Graduate*. After that success they were falling over themselves to give him money. It was never like that after I'd made *Kane* and *The Ambersons*, they never made money.'

The film continued on, take after take with no sound. As he talked, he was watching the material and working out exactly what he needed to do – off the cuff, instinctive. 'I tried to buy *Catch-22* but I couldn't put the finance together, even to buy the rights, let alone make the picture.'

He laughed to himself in the darkness. The film whirred on. 'He's a distant cousin of Einstein, you know.'

'Who?' I asked.

'Who the hell do you think? Nichols. His real name is Peschkowsky. He was born in Berlin and escaped to the US just before the war broke out, when he was a child.'

'He was one of the lucky ones.'

'No, not lucky. The fact is that many affluent Jews in Germany and Austria in the late 1930s, realising what was going on, began to emigrate. Hitler was happy for them to go. The problem was that it was only those with money who could go.'

Finally the film ran out and I stopped the machine running. Without the film running through the editing machine, the room was black, pitch black. I got up and went to the door. I couldn't find it. I was flailing about in the darkness trying to find the door handle. I was even pushing the wall hoping it was the door.

'Dorian. What are you doing?' came the voice.

'Trying to get out,' I replied lamely.

'Are we trapped in here?' he chortled.

'Hopefully not,' I said.

He struck a match and relit his soggy cigar. 'Can you see now?' he said kindly.

I found the door with the light of the match.

'Entombed with Orson Welles'! he exclaimed, 'Good name for a TV special!'

Mr Welles stood up and told me to contact Ann Rogers to tell her that he would need Laurence Harvey in Rome for some more shooting and that I would have to go to Vienna to collect some earlier footage which, for some unaccountable reason, had been left there. Probably some footage shot in Yugoslavia, which had been smuggled over the border into Austria.

With no further delay, Mr Welles, with me trotting eagerly behind, swept back to the Hotel Scribe, that discreet and old-fashioned establishment with brass-handled lifts, nineteenth-century French bourgeois furniture and concierges with bad consciences about their activities, or lack of them, in the Second World War.

★

'It's as if the First World War took the stuffing out of them and they simply didn't have the puff for a second round. On reflection, who can blame them after Verdun?'

The French Jockey Club had been founded here, Josephine Baker made it her home from home when she was performing in Paris, and, last but not least, the Lumière brothers had first presented their global screening near here in a room in the Grand Café with their cinematographe and its unique two-claw pull-down mechanism, which was really the first film camera and gave its name to the great industry of entertainment and information that followed.

If you were a war correspondent covering the Allied invasion of Europe in 1944, you had a dirty, exhausting and dangerous job – unless you worked out of the Hotel Scribe in Paris. The Scribe, in this instance aptly named, was Allied press headquarters after the liberation of Paris. It became a clearing house for all the war news that flowed from Europe as the Allied armies drove into Germany. In its comfortable rooms with hot baths, its restaurants at below black-market prices, and especially its mahogany-panelled basement bar, newsmen could be found at work and play. Through the Scribe's portals passed the cream of wartime journalism: Ernest Hemingway, George Orwell, William Saroyan, Edward R. Murrow, Irwin Shaw, Malcolm Muggeridge, William L. Shirer, and Robert Capa – as well as the foot soldiers of newspapers, magazines, wire services and film. They helped make the Scribe a story in itself with their incessant demands for news, their carping about military censorship, their complaints about headquarters staff, and their after-hours pleasures. Ronald Weber describes the fascinating scene behind the front lines as a time of high intensity in this gloriously open city.

★

In his suite filled with that wonderful aroma of Cuban cigars, Mr Welles planned the next moves of his European summer. After I had collected the extra material in Vienna, we would reconvene in Rome in four days to begin editing.

The feeling I had during this meeting, and at many subsequent meetings, was that I was in the presence of an immensely powerful man. He was a man who was Churchillian in proportion and mind, somehow wasted on these small personal projects, rather than on epic pictures, or more appropriately, matters of great political significance. As he sat there on his sofa holding his cigar in his left hand, new and unlit, or freshly burning, or old and soggy, he would play with his left ear with his left hand as he ruminated. He also did this whenever he paused for thought while typing page after page of his visual and literary imaginings.

'I don't take art as seriously as politics. I find these so-called experts on my work quite tedious. Looking for inner meanings and God knows what to fulfil their pseudo-intellectual efforts. God, how boring!'

People at the time and subsequently used to ask me what I thought Mr Welles should be, and I always responded by saying he should be President of the United States. Then his great knowledge and wisdom, his strength, energy, intelligence and his epic voice, ability to charm people, and even his ability to trick people, could all have been put to constructive use, rather than these endless fiddly projects of no great consequence that he worked on when I was with him. He was like a great painter in his studio, forever pulling out unfinished canvases and dabbling with them, then putting them back in the pile, somehow aware that it was not his best work and he could do better but lacking the will or wherewithal to do it.

Mr Welles was no ordinary man.

He told me at lunch once that the Democratic Party had urged him in 1948 to run for office as senator in the state of Wisconsin.

He didn't, and a gentleman named McCarthy became senator
and history might have been a little different if you don't follow
Tolstoy's theories. President Roosevelt had appointed him in 1942
to be his personal emissary to Latin America to persuade the
waverers to fall in on the Allied side. For that mission, he was
given ambassadorial rank and the title Ambassador of Goodwill
was coined.

Many years later, a dear friend of mine, Bob Mrazek, a young
Democrat Member of Congress, was introduced to President Reagan
at a White House reception.

'And how did you start out in politics?' enquired the genial president.

Bob replied, 'Working for Senator McCarthy in his campaign.'

Reagan smiled and said, 'Good for you,' not realising my friend,
an idealistic young Democrat, had been working for the liberal
Eugene McCarthy in his abortive run in 1972 against Nixon and
not for the infamous McCarthy and his ludicrous witch-hunts!

In changed circumstances, Reagan might not have been the first
actor to end up as president.

★

'It was late 1944, the war was drawing to a close and President
Roosevelt was seeking a historic third term. It was the most
important work I was ever engaged in. To ensure that Roosevelt
was returned to the White House and that no deals were done
with the Nazis or the Japanese Imperialists. I even labelled the
Republicans 'the partisans of privilege.' I spent a lot of time
in the White House. I embellished the Fala story, which you
probably know.'

Mr Welles was talking to Oja, a Yugoslav born probably just
before the war, and me, an Englishman born at the end of the
war. How on earth might we know anything about the Fala story?

'It means "thank you" in Serbo-Croat,' Oja suggested.

'No,' said Mr Welles, 'It was the name of his little Scottie dog,
whom he adored. Fala is an abbreviation of some Scottish place.'

'And?' said Oja impatiently.

'Well, what happened was this. FDR was visiting the Aleutians, some godforsaken islands off the coast of Alaska.'

'Who's FDR?' enquired Oja.

'Franklin Delano Roosevelt,' I answered.

Mr Welles caught my eye but didn't draw breath.

'The story goes that Fala was left behind and that the president ordered a US warship to go back to the islands and recover the dog. I would have done the same damned thing. Unfortunately, the story got out and during that 1944 election the Republicans made a meal of it, accusing FDR of wasting millions of dollars of federal funds on saving a dog. When the president told me of this, I told him to turn it around into a speech mocking the Republicans. The gist of it was that OK, they could attack him, or his wife, or his family, but not his dog. Had they nothing better to do than attack his dog in this time of national emergency? So, by mocking the Republicans, we turned the whole thing in our favour! I was proud of that.'

He stirred in his chair and played with his ear. He was back in 1944, a young man of 29 again, with influence in the White House. His thought process was clearly whirring, 'Do you know, in the Battle of the Bulge, which took place only a few weeks later, the GIs in their foxholes, when they were being overrun by the German counter-attack, used the name "Fala" as their code word to identify friend or foe.'

As we walked out of the restaurant, Mr Welles said under his breath, 'I believe Roosevelt was truly one of our three or four great presidents up there with Lincoln and Washington.'

After recovering from illness, Welles accompanied Roosevelt to a rally in Boston's Fenway Park, where Frank Sinatra sang 'America the Beautiful' to his usual cheers from teenage girls. 'The crowd roared its enthusiasm as Orson Welles and Frank Sinatra were introduced,' reported the *Boston Globe,* which referred to the two stars as 'the dramatic voice' and 'The Voice.'

Welles, his anti-elite rhetoric as sharp as ever, claimed that the Republicans were running an entirely negative campaign. 'By free enterprise they want exclusive right to freedom,' he argued. 'They are stupid enough to think that a few can enjoy prosperity at the expense of the rest.' Welles kept campaigning up to election eve, when he delivered a nationally broadcast radio speech on a Democratic National Committee programme.

Impressed with Welles' oratory, Roosevelt suggested that the actor might have a future in politics. Welles, who had ambitions of running for office, was delighted. He would later tell people that, encouraged by Roosevelt, he'd contemplated running against US Senator Joe McCarthy in his native Wisconsin in 1946.

Roosevelt may have been flattering, but some biographers have another take. They characterise Welles' senatorial daydreams of 1944 as a sign of vanity, and his eloquence on Roosevelt's behalf as too high-minded to succeed from the mouth of a candidate himself. 'He was devout about great times needing great men,' wrote David Thomson in *Rosebud: The Story of Orson Welles*. 'So, he missed that drab, sly, common touch that gets elected.'

Still, Roosevelt appreciated Welles' oratory, and the connections between theatrical and political performance. After the election, in which Roosevelt beat Dewey 53 per cent to 46 per cent in the popular vote and 432–99 in the electoral vote, Roosevelt met with Welles once more. He also sent Welles another telegram, thanking him for his help with the campaign. 'It was a great show,' Roosevelt cabled, 'in which you played a great part.'

★

'My best performance was as Clarence Darrow in Compulsion. *I could perform like an actor on the stage which, after all, is what good attorneys are. I was only there a little over a week. On the last day, Zanuck walked up to me, thanked me, and told me my whole fee had been seized by the IRS. Can you believe it? But I won the Best Actor Award at Cannes!'*

9

Vienna and Harry Lime

So, I boarded a night train for Vienna, travelling first class which, according to Mr Welles, was the smart way to travel around Europe without being troubled by Customs, an essential prerequisite for moving large quantities of film from one country to another with-out paying duty taxes, a thing he was not keen to do since he didn't have any money in the first place. 'You will cross the borders during the night and the Customs men just check the passports of those sleeping in first class, they never check their luggage.'

How he kept himself afloat over all those years, and even in his final years in the States, was always a mystery to me – or a miracle. Or a torture, which only he could endure. Maybe he had sold his soul to the Devil all those years before, but he hardly deserved the cruelty that was meted out to him. Talk about singing for your supper; he did that in spade loads and the people responsible for his struggle with money should hang their heads in shame and cease calling him 'Orson' after one telephone call, and not pretend that they knew him, or had met him, or had tried to work with him even though he was 'difficult.' How could they claim he was unreliable when they never gave him a dime and had never worked with him in the first place?

I would have given him millions if I had had them, and he knew a lot of people with millions. Why didn't they help him? I will never know. First, he needed money to live, and second, to make movies. By denying him proper funding the world lost years of his unique creativity. Unlike an impoverished painter in some top-floor garret in Paris in the nineteenth century, or a starving writer in Russia at the turn of the century, he needed money to make film, to buy Kodak raw stock, to pay technicians, hire locations and equipment, and to pay actors. Painters need just paint and canvases, writers ink and paper. Movie-makers need more.

There was still snow in Vienna that spring, but I was able to retrieve the film from the safety vault in his name as well as any character from *The Third Man.*

Many years later, Mr Welles was in my thoughts when I had dinner with a distinguished academic sometimes, I think wrongly, suspected of being the 'Fourth Man.' As the conversation flowed, I remarked on the exquisite pair of candlesticks he sported on his sideboard.

'Oh, those,' he replied urbanely, 'they were given to me by Guy Burgess for allowing him to stay up an extra year at Cambridge.'

I nearly choked on my asparagus soup.

Guy Burgess was the Burgess of the notorious Burgess and Maclean, who had betrayed England to the Russians during the Cold War and fled to Russia to save their skins and lived out their years in exile there. Kim Philby was to follow them.

★

I walked the streets of the city waiting for my return night train and walked into the Museum of Ethnology. In the fading afternoon light, I found the feathers of King Montezuma and gazed at them. Was this the crown of Montezuma? Was this the trophy that proud Cortés brought back to Spain? Such a small, delicate object, stained by the sweat of an Aztec king as he faced the sinister and unforgiving conquistadors. Why was it that after 1,000 years he was the one of his dynasty thrown into this catastrophe? Maybe the Emperor Franz Joseph had seen it, little knowing that he too was marked by fate to be 'the last.'

Once again, my thoughts faded back to Mr Welles, who seemed to also carry that stigma: things would never be the same again after he had gone, and he belonged, in a sense, to another time. After leaving the museum, I wandered the streets of old Vienna, many of which had been used in *The Third Man*. The screenplay had been written by Grahame Greene, and was about that strange period after the war when Vienna was a divided city on the frontier of the East and West spying activities, and when the smuggling of black-market goods was rife.

His performance as Harry Lime was almost the defining film for Orson Welles the actor, and many wrongly credit him as director: 'I was only there a week, for God's sake. Shooting in those sewers was no fun. Though I do claim I occasionally altered Carol's camera angles. I always thought *Odd Man Out* was a better picture. More to the script and James Mason was outstanding as that mortally wounded IRA gunman on the run. Extraordinary.'

Just a week, forever remembered.

'And I did improvise that speech of Lime after the scene on the Ferris wheel, you know, the one about cuckoo clocks. I'd heard it somewhere before and thought it would work. It did, though someone wrote to me later telling me that the cuckoo clock was a German invention from the Black Forest and not Swiss at all!' He roared with laughter.

I suddenly said, 'And at the time of the Borgias, during the high Renaissance, the most feared mercenary soldiers in Europe were the Swiss regiments.'

'So that whole speech is a lot of hokum!'

For a moment I thought he was going to explode with rage at my pointing out a further factual inaccuracy. Instead, he toyed with his cigar and took a thoughtful puff.

'It worked brilliantly, anyway,' I said.

'Exactly,' said Oja, wanting to placate him.

He laughed, 'It just shows as long as the delivery has enough hutzpah, you can say anything and it works!'

★

Rome in the spring with flowers in terracotta pots all down both sides of the Spanish Steps. Did John Keats smell them as he struggled with his awful last breaths?

Mr Welles was the owner of two Steenbeck flatbed editing machines. These were hugely expensive machines and must have cost him considerable amounts of money to buy. I think his idea was, at some point, to place them in a house he owned so that we could work privately on his projects. These flatbed machines enabled the 35mm film and the 35mm magnetic soundtrack to roll through the synchronised rollers horizontally. To run sound and picture, you synchronised them by placing the clapperboard closed shot with the sound of the 'clap' – hence the clapperboard's use at the beginning of takes. Running forward from there would ensure that sound and picture were in sync.

The vertical method of editing film used in the UK and the States was usually at that time with the Moviola machine, which Mr Welles disliked: 'I can't see the damned picture I've shot if I'm looking over the shoulder of the editor. With this machine, I can see with anyone I'm working with what we are doing and on the second machine I put my new rushes which I can select and check if it's going to fit into the picture.'

He used this method all the time, since he was always shooting new stuff and incorporating it into unfinished material he had shot before, maybe last week, maybe last year, and maybe even some years before.

Anyway, after my training with Lucidi and son, I got the drift and positioned the machines in a rather dark and cramped editing room at Fono Roma, one of the leading post-production houses, situated just off the Piazza del Popolo near the Porta Flaminia in the Aurelian Walls.

Rome in the 1960s was very much the European base for Hollywood, and a number of pleasant light comedies were produced there, as well as various historical epics and, of course, the spaghetti westerns which made Clint Eastwood into a major star and Sergio Leone a major director back in the US. It was at this time that the seemingly perennial Dino de Laurentiis began to make a name for himself.

We had a plump Italian editing assistant called Cecilia, to whom I used to sing Simon and Garfunkel every morning. She had no grasp of what I meant by 'breaking my heart and shaking my confidence daily.' She was no Sophia Loren, anyway, so it didn't matter.

Mr Welles' method of editing was to have the edited version of the film, in this case *The Deep*, on one edit machine and the new rushes (dailies) on the other. We would run through the new material and make it into two rolls, one rejects and one possibles. The possible roll would then be moved onto the editing machine and inserted into the actual cut. Pretty logical, really.

This went on for a few days until Mr Welles was comfortable. One morning an employee came into our cutting room and asked us a technical question in Italian. Mr Welles struggled to answer perfectly and I managed to sort out the problem. 'I'm not as good a linguist as I'm made out to be,' he apologised to me. He didn't mention that his Italian was pretty darned good, as was his French and Spanish.

He was staying at the Hotel Eden during this time, a discreet luxury hotel at the bottom of a discreet side street off the Via Veneto. Every morning I would drive in my Austin Mini to pick him up at the hotel. The hotel porters would turn up their noses as my modest, and extremely small, two-door automobile arrived. As Mr Welles swept out of the lobby, dressed all in black and carrying his usual baggage of a script or notebook and Havana box, they would visibly choke at what was about to happen. I would rush round to the passenger door and hold it open as Welles literally dropped into the passenger seat and swung his legs into the car. I should point out that I always parked in the crown of the street rather than near the curb, where the angle of the car door might totally preclude the possibility of closing the door once it was jammed on the pavement by the weight of Mr Welles in the car.

Once he was wedged in, I would force the door closed as gently as possible so as not to bruise his left thigh, then rush round and jump into the driver's seat, leaning excessively to my right so that I wasn't pushed into his ample lap. I would then start the engine and reach for the gearstick which was, by this time, stuck somewhere underneath the right part of Welles' body and clothes. Having engaged first gear to at least give the vehicle some chance of achieving momentum, I often, out of politeness, dispensed with second gear and moved straight to third, hoping that I had enough speed.

Mr Welles remained silent during these complex machinations, puffing on his cigar, and once we were moving he would think and breathe noisily while I would wait for him to speak, as all polite young people are taught to do – only speak when you are spoken to.

At our destination, reached through the wall of cigar smoke that filled the little car, the same ritual would be followed in reverse, although I would always ensure that where I parked there was room for him to throw his weight outwards and downwards from the car, with space beyond for him to get into an upright position. He always managed this manoeuvre very adeptly. It was normally accompanied by the casting away of the first cigar of the day, which had been finished in the car.

Once a passer-by leapt forward and snatched up the smouldering cigar. When I asked what he was doing, the passer-by replied, in Italian, 'But it's the cigar of Orson Welles! I will keep it forever!'

★

'George Peppard is a pain in the ass. He took himself too seriously on House of Cards. *He had no sense of humour and was always trying get approval. Thank God, I've only been in one picture with him. I continually had to reassure him that he was great. And he wasn't!'*

10

OSTIA AND LAURENCE HARVEY

I peered closely at the SPQR letters carved in the marble stone: the ancient acronym for *Senātus Populusque Rōmānus*, 'the Senate and People of Rome.' Those same letters had been engraved on the standards of the Roman legions as they marched into battle. And they still appeared on the manhole covers and gutters of Rome, as though to remind us of former glories.

Around me were the ruins of Ostia, Rome's ancient port, where grain from the Empire had been brought by galleys across the Mediterranean from Alexandria and Carthage to feed the citizens of Rome. Acres of broken arches, random columns, colonnades, cobbled streets and the obligatory amphitheatre stretched before me like a Piranesi lithograph, but for the green, grassy unexcavated mounds dotted with the darker green of vertical cypress trees and green porridge stone pines. It was as if the trees were fertilised by the long-dead inhabitants of this long-dead city.

'I've flown Larry Harvey out to dub some of his lines and we need to do a couple of pick-up shots we can insert in the edit. We need a yacht, a nice old wooden yacht to match our location material from Yugoslavia.' So, I had driven down to Ostia with the clips from the shot footage and negotiated with the owner to use his yacht's cockpit and wheel as the matching location for the pick-up shots of Laurence Harvey. My visit to the ruins had taken place as I was waiting for Mr Welles and Mr Harvey to arrive.

Laurence Harvey was a big star then. He had an unsavoury arrogance about him, like a spiv with his smooth-toned voice, almost too perfect for the slightly devious features. He was a Lithuanian Jew, whose family had emigrated to South Africa just before the horrors unfolded in the Baltic States. Harvey had made his way to London and enrolled for a while at the Royal Academy of Dramatic Art – hence his urbane English upmarket voice.

He had an 'I don't really give a shit about anything' kind of aura about him. He wasn't particularly likeable. He had had an Oscar nomination for *Room at the Top* and had broken into Hollywood with a number of films, in particular *The Alamo*, where he had formed an unlikely friendship with John Wayne. He and Mr Welles had first met on the set of *The Black Rose* in the 1950s.

Sadly, we were shooting, not aboard one of those Roman galleys belonging to the *Senātus Populusque Rōmānus* but on this old yacht crying out for some new varnish. Mr Welles, me and Laurence Harvey – three men on a boat, plus a small film crew. We achieved the required shots and drove over to lunch at a trattoria in the countryside near the Via Appia.

'Do you remember that scene shot in Morocco when they hung those bodies in the background?'

'Actual bodies?' I gasped.

'My God, yes. They later told me that the French colonel who was in charge of operations against nationalists in those days shot some terrorists or freedom fighters and offered them to the people in charge of the set since apparently he was a fan of Orson Welles.' Harvey sniggered as though the corpses he remembered were of no importance.

Mr Welles looked horrified and, scowling a little, mumbled, 'I have no recollection of that.'

'You were too drunk at the time,' sneered Harvey.

'With good reason, it was such a crappy film.'

Over dinner in Frascati we talked about Harry Cohn, Darryl Zanuck and Hollywood moguls in general. The lights of Rome flickered in the distance.

'What about Harry Cohn?' asked Harvey.

Mr Welles was happy to oblige:

'We were short of money for my theatre production of *Around the World in 80 Days*, so I called Harry Cohn in Hollywood. "I have a great story for you if you could send me $50,000 by return in one hour. I'll sign a contract to make it."

'"What story?" asked Cohn.

'I was calling from a payphone, and luckily next to it was a display of paperbacks. I gave him the title of one of them, *Lady from Shanghai*.

'"Buy the novel and I'll make the film!" I screamed. I was running out of money in the payphone.

'An hour later, I got the money, we financed the play and I ended up directing *Lady from Shanghai*, which was a diabolical book. My movie wasn't much better.

'You know Zanuck, that little midget, wasn't Jewish at all. Not one ounce. But he operated in a very Jewish world and was successful. He even made a movie about a Gentile pretending to be a Jew with Gregory Peck. He was Swiss from godforsaken Nebraska. He was ruined by that ridiculous obsession he had for the talentless Juliette Greco. How can these great men be brought so low by the needs of their genitals?'

I looked at Laurence Harvey and he looked back at me, then I looked at Mr Welles and he held my look for a moment but never wavered.

The next day, we went to Fono Roma to dub Laurence Harvey's voice onto the picture we had shot the previous day and some of the material shot the previous summer before I joined Mr Welles.

★

I should explain dubbing. It is the process when you put the voices onto the picture after it has been filmed. In most motion pictures and TV series nowadays, sound is taken during the filming, either by means of the boom microphone on the end of a pole held above the actors by the assistant soundman (boom operator) or with concealed radio microphones which are clipped on clothing as near as possible to the actor's mouth. Only occasionally is dubbing necessary when the sound quality originally recorded is not good enough or when subtle script changes are needed.

In the US and UK, the bell and red light in the studio is respected and silence falls immediately. But in Italy there is a problem with taking sound on a film set. The problem is this. Asking one Italian to stop speaking for a moment is one thing. Asking two or more Italians to stop talking for any length of time is a sheer impossibility. In fact, it borders on cruelty. I think movie producers shooting in Italy realised this early on and gave up trying. To be honest, shooting without quality sound does quicken up the filming process since it is one less element to look for in a given 'take,' but what it incurs is the dubbing process where a short piece of film is 'looped' for the actor with a line drawn across the picture to queue him or her. Some actors are very good at it: indeed, there are professional dubbing artists who specialise in 'voicing,' particularly foreign-language versions of films. Hence an Italian movie can, with intelligent translation, be dubbed into French or Spanish, for example, without too much trouble.

The only good Italian sound recordist I worked with was Vittorio Trentino who, despite his age, later worked on *The Damned* and *Death in Venice*. We used him on sound for *The Merchant of Venice* sequences we shot, but he would always get exasperated by Mr Welles' somewhat cavalier attitude to sound recording on set. I think because of his guerrilla style of filmmaking, he felt that a cumbersome blimped camera would merely slow things down and anyway he could always dub tracks on later. Looking back at his work, you can say that his attitude to sound recording was not as it should have been. Sound design and music are now such an important part of the film-making process that sometimes his work can be criticised in this respect.

★

Back to Mr Welles, Laurence Harvey and me in the dubbing theatre. There was Laurence at the microphone, Mr Welles directing in the darkness and me checking the synchronisation.

'Was that OK, Dorian?' called Mr Welles.

'Fine,' was my mumbled reply, when asked to comment on a line spoken immaculately by one of England's finest Shakespearian actors and directed by the most famous film director in the world.

'What?' persisted Mr Welles.

'Fine,' I repeated, mesmerised by their two silhouettes – Welles, a giant looming figure; Harvey, the aquiline profile.

'Just fine?' Mr Welles queried, and roared with laughter as only he could laugh. 'You think Laurence Harvey is only fine?'

'No, good,' I stuttered, 'very good.'

'Larry, he thinks you're good!' roared Mr Welles.

'Thank you, Dorian,' bowed the smarmy Harvey, putting me out of my misery, and we went on to the next line.

They say that one of the reasons Mr Welles didn't ever finish *The Deep* was because Laurence Harvey died in 1973. I don't think that had anything to do with it. I think he had long since got bored with it and sensed it wasn't going to work. If you think about the screenplay and even the material he shot, it somehow never looked like an Orson Welles film. Maybe it was the fact it was shot in Technicolor. Maybe the canvas he was painting was not big enough for him, or the raw material meaningful enough for him. It was as though the weight of the material was too light for him, a man who always seemed to grasp innuendo and inference, and that he found these characters too facile.

'Have you ever heard of a man called Nikola Tesla? Probably the greatest scientist of the twentieth century. Greater than Edison and all the rest of them.'

   I never had and, in those days, there was no Wikipedia, so I never did.

11

JOHN HUSTON

'I want you to go to London,' he said, 'and bring me some cigars.'

'When?' I asked.

'Today,' he said. 'Now.'

'And return?'

'Today. This afternoon.'

I duly went to Leonardo da Vinci Airport – only the Italians could name their most important airport after a famous painter – travelled to London, picked up the Montecristos in the cigar room of Alfred Dunhill, returned to the airport and flew back to Rome that afternoon. I then drove directly to Cinecittà, where Mr Welles was acting in John Huston's film *The Kremlin Letter*, as senior Soviet official Bresnavitch.

I found Mr Welles in his dressing room and handed him his box of cigars.

'Dorian, you are a hero. I was running short and I couldn't suffer the humiliation of having to ask John if I could have one of his!' He chortled at his own remark.

Then Huston walked in. Mr Welles introduced me. Here I was, in a cramped dressing room in Cinecittà – I remember most rooms that Mr Welles inhabited seemed to get smaller – with the legendary John Huston and the legendary Orson Welles. If I had been a movie fan, or an aspiring director, I would have thought I had died and gone to heaven – and I was, so I did.

These two giant figures of the cinema, both mavericks with the lines of their lives written on their faces, talked seriously about the scene they were about to shoot.

'Let's do this now and go to dinner,' suggested Huston.

'A good idea. Dorian has had a long day getting my cigars!'

We made our way onto the brightly lit studio set and they smoothly and efficiently did their thing. Silence was called, the red light on, the scene and take number called by the clapper boy and Huston quietly said, 'Action.' Mr Welles slipped into his pseudo-Russian accent and phrased his lines perfectly. These were two professionals at work. They did three takes, Huston liked the third, and that was it. It was a wrap for the day.

In those days, the director had no way of knowing how good a take was. There was no simultaneous video playback to check takes. The only person who 'saw' the take was the camera operator with his eye to the eyepiece. The director just relied on his judgement and instinct, and Huston and Welles had pretty good judgement on the quality of a particular shot.

At dinner that night I sat with these two legendary, Hemingwayesque figures. They had both had their run-ins with Hollywood, but Huston seemed to have survived better. Their careers had intertwined many times. Huston had directed *Moby Dick* with Mr Welles as Father Mapple; Welles had written the script. Welles had directed *The Stranger* when Huston had to turn it down, twenty-five years before they both had had films up for Oscars in a number of categories – Welles for *Citizen Kane*, Huston for *The Maltese Falcon*. Huston had made more Hollywood mainstream pictures, including *The Treasure of the Sierra Madre*, *The Asphalt Jungle*, *The African Queen*, *Moby Dick* and, more recently, *The Night of the Iguana*, with Richard Burton and Ava Gardner. They had both made fleeting contributions to the disastrous satire that was *Casino Royale* two years before, yet another example of Hollywood misreading and ruining a brilliantly exciting book for its ruthless financial ends.

We talked about fox hunting in Ireland and his own pack of hounds, the Galway Blazers. Mr Welles seemed surprised that

I knew anything about the manners and etiquette of fox hunting. The evening ended with two great men remembering *Beat the Devil*, which Huston had directed on the Amalfi coast and where he had been visited by Mr Welles. They laughed when Huston told Mr Welles that Truman Capote, who had written the script, was petrified at the prospect of meeting the legendary Orson Welles.

'How could he be afraid of me?' roared Mr Welles.

'Because, Orson,' replied Huston in his mellifluous tones, part American, part Irish, 'you are a formidable man with a very loud voice, strong opinions and a wicked sense of humour. Most people are scared of you.'

Mr Welles looked a little taken aback, then swigged another mouthful of cognac. Fortified, he then relished the thought. 'I'm just a honey, really! Putty in the right person's hands.'

At that moment, with Mr Welles playing 'vulnerable,' he did look like a gigantic baby. Come to think of it, he must have been a very splendid baby and doubtless his mother, Beatrice, must have doted on him. She certainly did during his childhood and early teenage years. From there came his enormous self-confidence and character devoid of self-doubt.º

'Bullshit,' scoffed Huston, and he grinned his particular grin with his teeth showing like a benevolent carnivorous predator.

We drank more cognac before returning home. Mr Welles was staying at the Hilton and I drove him there. 'Come in with me,' he instructed as I parked. He clearly had had a little too much cognac. He staggered slowly, always dignified, into the lobby and we got to the lifts. There was one available and we got in alone. He was leaning against the rail as I pressed the floor number. As the lift ascended, he began to slip down the side he was leaning on. I leapt across and succeeded in holding his not-inconsiderable weight by pinning him against the side. But, in using all my strength to keep him upright I was pressing hard against his stomach and this caused his trousers to slowly slip down from his waist. The more I pushed, the narrower his waist became, so the inevitable happened.

Picture it for a moment – me pinning Mr Welles, this huge man, against a wall to keep him vertical, and his trousers were slipping down …

At this point the lift arrived at its designated floor and the doors opened. Staring at us were two very elderly Italian nuns, obviously on a visit to the Vatican, which was very close by. Their mouths fell open as I apologised pathetically and Mr Welles hitched up his trousers, collected himself, and walked with great dignity to his room.

The next day nothing was mentioned of our adventure.

Another lunch at Mama Rosa's, a wonderful trattoria just off the Via Veneto, and at another table sits Robert Culp who comes over and has a friendly and amusing conversation with Mr Welles. He's probably one of the most recognisable stars in the world at the moment, since the incredibly popular TV series I Spy *with Bill Cosby. He also writes many of the episodes.*

Mr Welles introduces me to the delights of bolito mixto, that simple king of Italian medieval dishes, and young semi-sparkling red Italian wine.

Yet another lunch at Mama Rosa's. Welles draws a picture of me with glasses and my hair frizzed up, denoting nervous tension. We all laugh and I keep the drawing.

12

The Tyrrhenian Coast

In June, we drove up to Livorno on the Tyrrhenian Sea to the famous Tirrenia Film Studios. Filoteo Alberini made the first Italian movie there, *La Presa di Roma*, about the entry of Garibaldi's troops into Rome during the Risorgimento.

The studios, now in decline, had offered Mr Welles very economic terms to film and edit there. He politely listened, but seemed to have no intention of taking up their offer. I suspect he was looking for cheaper editing facilities than at Fono Roma and a cheaper hotel than the Eden in Rome. An added incentive was the fact that Livorno had a small area of canals which could double for Venice.

One morning, Mr Welles decided to go to Pisa to show Oja. It was cloudy, but still the central Piazza del Duomo was stunning with its green lawns contrasting so vividly with the white marble of the Duomo, the Leaning Tower and the Baptistry. Then we drove down to the sea towards Viareggio and its vast beach where Shelley's body had been washed ashore.

'Come on, Dorian, take us there. You're always telling me about this great romance of Byron and Shelley in Italy.'

It was raining as we got out of the car, Oja remained put, and together we staggered down to the water's edge. We stood there with the wind blowing Mr Welles' black hat so he had to hold on to it, the rain in our faces and his cape flaring out behind. He looked like some Old Testament prophet.

Suddenly he began to recite *King Lear*:

Blow, winds, and crack your cheeks! Rage! Blow!
You cataracts and hurricanes, spout
Till you have drench'd our steeples, drown'd the cocks!
You sulphurous and thought-executing fires,
Vaunt-couriers to oak-cleaving thunderbolts,
Singe my white head! And thou, all-shaking thunder,
Strike flat the thick rotundity o' the world!
Crack nature's moulds, all germens spill at once.

By chance, I had done *King Lear* during my last year at school and had played the Fool in the school play. So I went for it:

O nuncle, court holy-water in a dry house is better than this rain-water out o'door.
Good nuncle, in, and ask thy daughters' blessing; here's a night pities neither wise man nor fool.

Mr Welles ranted on:

Blow winds and crack your cheeks! Rage! Blow!
You cataracts and hurricanes, spout
Till you have drench'd our steeples, drown'd the cocks!

His magnificent voice answered the distant thunder across the Tyrrhenian Sea and I knew at that moment that I was the only witness to his performance.

As we walked back to the car we reminisced about Shelley lying drowned on that very beach, about Byron riding out from Pisa to witness the burning of his friend's body on a pagan funeral pyre and his heart snatched from the fiery embers by the darkly bearded Cornish adventurer, Edward Trelawny.

'His ashes and the remains of Keats are buried in the Protestant cemetery near the Aurelian Walls of Rome near Porta San Paolo. My ashes will go elsewhere,' he mused.

★

Mrs Rogers came out to Livorno bearing wads of cash for Mr Welles to survive on for a few more weeks. She stayed a few days, and we all went out for lunch to a trattoria near the port. Mr Welles and Oja teased her a little, which she took in good grace.

'I'll have you know, Mr Welles, that this place was called Leghorn in the eighteenth century by the Royal Navy and was one of our main points of replenishment in the Mediterranean. Lord Nelson and many of his captains were familiar with this place.'

'And the women, I suspect,' laughed Mr Welles. And Oja laughed along with him. Ann Rogers, or Wanda, as they called her behind her back for some reason, looked disapproving.

'She always reminded me of my housekeeper in Hollywood, Dorothy Holmes, always fretting and worrying about me. She was English as well, and a brilliant cook. I adored her.'

'A brilliant English cook?' queried Oja, 'Does such a thing exist?'

Mr Welles ignored the comment.

13

Risorgimento Discord

Back in Rome the next week, it was very hot and humid and we spent a long and tedious day in the cutting room. The hours had been pretty fruitless, with endless changes and changes of changes. I was fed up. Alessandro Tasca, who had dropped in, had just left.

On the way back in the car, cigar smoke nearly choking me, Mr Welles said how important a role the aristocracy played in creating the modern Italian state. Without thinking, I threw in the comment, 'But they didn't do much to help during the Risorgimento, to make Italy an independent state. It was Garibaldi and Cavour and Mazzini who really drove it forward with the backing of the people.'

'What the hell do you know about the Italian Risorgimento?' Mr Welles exploded, as only he could explode. And we were in a small stifling car with no air-conditioning so the explosion was infinitely more deadly. As he roared he seemed to get even bigger and he boomed out his displeasure at me like an enraged bull elephant.

'What crap!' he bellowed. 'What the hell would you know about it?'

In for a penny, I concluded, in for a pound. Sod it. 'Well, I specialised in the subject at school,' I replied sulkily, realising that if I didn't stand my ground now I would be annihilated forever. The word 'school' sounded pathetic.

'And what did you learn at school, young man?' he breathed sarcastically. 'Your privileged upper-class school, which the English are so impressed by?'

'That the Italian aristocracy, be they from the Austrian-occupied northern states, the Papal States or the Bourbon kingdom, basically sat back and watched Italy achieve its nationhood without them.'

I had foolishly forgotten that Mr Welles' wife, Paola Mori, from whom he had never divorced despite his long-term relationship with Oja, was actually Paola di Girifalco, Contessa di Girifalco, a true blue Italian aristocrat.

'You don't know what you're talking about,' he mocked.

'But I do,' I insisted, going for broke. 'Mazzini, Ricasoli, Garibaldi were not members of the aristocracy.'

'So what?' he choked back at me.

We had arrived back at the hotel and this time he threw open the door of my car and launched himself out, almost falling flat on his face. I got out and was about to call it a day. There was very little oxygen in my lungs after the drive from the studio, which had been like being on the inside of the engine of an air conditioner.

'No!' howled Mr Welles at me, 'I haven't finished with you yet, come with me.'

And he stormed into the hotel. I followed like a lamb to the slaughter. The concierge and porters and guests of this very sedate hotel were frozen in fascination at the ranting of the great man.

The lift of the Hotel Eden at that time was one of those very small and ancient brass and glass lifts with an old gate that pulled across to close it. It barely had room for two people at a time, let alone Mr Welles. Oja, who had been waiting in the lobby, came over and attempted to calm him. He shrugged her off. So, four of us got in the lift as the argument continued, Mr Welles and Oja, the unfortunate porter who drove the lift, and the even more unfortunate me. I ended up facing Mr Welles' upper stomach and lower chest, heaving with anger and noise from his diatribe against me, as we rose up through the lobby to the upper floors.

The last glimpse I had of the lobby was of concerned faces all looking and watching us noisily disappear into the upper reaches of the hotel. I began to wonder what in the hell I knew about European history – a relatively youthful Englishman, who hardly had a command of the Italian language. I was far too young to be pontificating on such matters, and anyway, who cared what I thought about anything?

The rampage roared on as we entered his suite until he finally dismissed me, like some king with an unfortunate servant. I slid back through the hotel lobby grinning sheepishly at the porters while they and their guests just stared at me with their astonished mouths still open from the earlier barrage. Mr Welles in full throat was an impressive sight and sound, combining the volume of Pavarotti with the timbre of Paul Robeson and the physical presence of the Incredible Hulk. No wonder they stared at me. I think they were amazed I was still alive.

The following morning, it was drizzling as he fell into my little car. He graciously apologised for the harsh words of the previous evening and conceded that perhaps I was right, or he was right, but we were still friends.

I agreed.

Then he said something to me that I will never forget:

'Dorian, friendship is very important. We're born alone and we die alone. In between those two moments, with love and friendship we create the illusion that we're not alone.'

Straight from the horse's mouth. I was stunned into silence as I gripped the steering wheel more tightly, my tyres screaming on the shining wet surface of the paving stones around the looming Colosseum of three mighty emperors, Vespasian, Titus and Domitian.

14

A History of Bullfighting

Mr Welles was continually writing screenplays, bashing away on his old typewriter normally placed on a coffee table in front of a sofa. I have often wondered where they all are now, those brain-children of his tempestuous, imaginative magician's mind. They were for current productions such as *The Deep* or *Don Quixote*, another piece of work he never finished, or future planned projects such as the screenplay about the American journalist and the young Spanish matador – the old bull and the young bull, the man of experience who had seen it all, and the young maestro with all the natural talent and, above all, that priceless gift of youth which the older man could never regain. It is something I have thought about many times since those days, the unawareness of the priceless gift of youth and its seamless drift into the later ages of man. I think this scenario eventually became his last, disastrous effort, *The Other Side of the Wind*, with him directing John Huston who was playing a character who was part Welles and part Hemingway.

★

We were sitting on the terrace of the Cipriani in Venice taking morning coffee. The night before we had been in Harry's Bar.

'God, Hemingway spent money in that place. A lot of money. He was a drunk by then and if you're a drunk the last place you want to drink is Harry's Bar! You'll become a drunk and a bankrupt!' He

roared with laughter and relit his cigar. 'He was a good friend. The
first time we came across each other was in a recording studio in
New York. I was just a stage actor then and made extra money doing
voiceovers for documentaries and commercials.

'Anyway, I was recording a documentary about the Spanish Civil
War. The script had been written by Hemingway. I didn't like it and
began to make changes and criticisms. I didn't realise that in the
darkness Hemingway had snuck into the studio to watch what was
going on. Eventually I stood up and said, "This has to be rewrit-
ten". Hemingway stood up and told me I was reading it like goddam
Shakespeare and the way I pronounced "infantry" was obscene.
I don't know what the hell he was talking about. He'd drunk a bit
and so had I. I'd spent the whole day in the theatre fuelled by demon
drink. We ended up rolling around the floor wrestling. I was angry,
he was angry. They pulled us apart and we became friends over a
bottle of whisky.'

★

The idea of the young bullfighter in his prime followed by an
ageing film director was his idea. The young bullfighter as a young
artist in his prime, immersed in the mystery that is the *corrida*,
with its ancient roots in Mediterranean and Middle Eastern culture, pursuing his 'sacred beasts' and their 'death in the afternoon.'
And Mr Welles would be the ageing director – who else?

Years later, he adapted this to the more pedestrian concept of
an ageing film director trying to make one last picture as more
youthful directors superseded him: a miserable cop-out from his
original dream with all its visceral drama and potentially remarkable cinematography.

If it had been produced, it would have made a wonderful
postscript to his melodramatic life rather than the disorganised
pieces of ill-thought-out, half-finished, tawdry Americana photographed by an ex-pornographer that he released before he died,
like the blotched half-finished sketches of a great artist, with giant

canvases leaning against his studio walls, empty and waiting to be worked on. Someone even told me that he had paid one of the crew with his *Citizen Kane* Oscar.

Oh, what a fall was there. And a few blocks away the big stars and producers in their self-righteous gilded palaces lauded him in chat shows and at celebrity roasts, wheeling him on like some witty dinosaur from a bygone age. Don Quixote, Captain Ahab and Sir John Falstaff all rolled into one.

Mr Welles had a theory on this, which I have, subsequently, called The Ten-Year Thing. It is completely the reverse of The Seamless Drift Theory. He said that people grew older by decades and each decade suddenly appeared on your face like the portrait of Dorian Gray. And the process was not gradual, but instant, particularly to the beholder.

I have applied this theory many times since, both with myself and with friends, and it works – people are suddenly 'in their thirties' or whatever, and it suddenly happens. The watersheds that mark these moments are rarely evident to the person to whom it is happening.

I had one such moment lying, almost naked, on an operating table with my arms, legs and head encased in metal restrainers, like when you make angels in deep snow as a child. The surgeon towered over me and told me that my heart was blocked and that he was going to have to saw through my chest bone, drag open my rib cage and somehow cut into my heart and splice new pipes into it, having cut them out of my legs, to enable me to live a while longer. Like a forerunning angel of death, he was telling me to my helpless face that my youth was ended and that a new chapter was about to begin.

When he left the dimly lit room, where we had been watching the inadequate beatings of my heart, I wept at my helplessness and for the intangible ghost of my youth that slipped from the room silently as the door gently closed, shutting out the light from the passage outside. My forebodings about the coming ritual, like an African coming-of-age rite in reverse, proved right.

'You know the great tragedy of Dominguín was that he was in love with his sister. Ordóñez, his great rival, married her. He never got over that. I am a great friend of Ordóñez. When I die I have arranged for my ashes to be buried on his farm outside Ronda.'

Apparently, Mr Welles had first gone to Spain when he was a teenager after his seminal trip to Ireland. 'One day you should drive round Ireland in your little car buying up all the pictures I painted for my suppers. Then wrap them up, take them back to New York and sell them for a fortune!'

This must have been in about 1931, before the Civil War had erupted. Hemingway had been in Spain during the 1920s and had become obsessed with the *corrida*.

'The rivalry of Dominguín and Ordóñez was the stuff of legend. Two great protagonists of their art form performing week after week, season after season, in their ballet of death.'

'Like Belmonte and Joselito,' I suggested.

Mr Welles drew on his newly lit cigar and enjoyed the moment. 'How on earth do you know about those two? They were a little before my time, though Hemingway mentions Belmonte in one of his novels, I think.'

'They were the greatest.'

'Please explain to me how a callow Anglo-Saxon boy comes to be an aficionado of the *corrida*. I am fascinated. Don't tell me, you wrote an essay on their contrasting styles and that got you into Oxford?'

Mr Welles was challenging me, but this time in a nice way, with affection. So I told him what I knew and how I knew it.

★

My father had travelled frequently to Spain in the fifties and, becoming enamoured of the *corrida*, took out a subscription for the bullfighting magazine, *El Ruedo*, replete with photographs and stories. That and *The Ring*, meaning the same thing but an American magazine about professional boxing, were my monthly fare at my preparatory school. They both arrived battered by the post, rolled up into a tube with their outer pages somewhat dog-eared. They showed two contrasting worlds of what I deemed heroism: brave men plying their trade in their chosen profession with raw courage, iron discipline and sheer artistry (or dogged determination, depending on their individual talents).

While Rocky Marciano, Sugar Ray Robinson and Carmen Basilio dazzled as modern-day gladiators where blood and sweat was the currency, I was a little more fascinated by the more exotic tight costumes and balletic moves of the matadors that I read about. Belmonte was the one for me.

Juan Belmonte Garcia, the underslung-jawed boy from Seville. Short, bow-legged and muscular, he seemed fearless, always standing motionless inches from the giant bulls' horns and often being gored. Writers who witnessed him said it was not the elegance or beauty of his *muleta* work, but the closeness of it and its unique rhythm. He would turn the bull left and right almost to a beat. They said that if you were outside the bullring and listened to the applause of the crowd it sounded like the rhythm of the waves. Three, four or five equal waves, then a larger one, ending with Belmonte striding away to gather his breath. It was literally breathtaking. Strangely, the golden age of these events took place when the First World War was raging and during its concluding peace conferences.

It was a golden age because Belmonte had a rival – Joselito. Joselito was the opposite of Belmonte. He was tall and elegant, with an aquiline nose, balletic in his movement, but equally brave. Week after week, in *ferias* across Spain, these two young men drove each other to heights of artistry never equalled, before or since. They were the Roger Federer and Rafael Nadal, the Mohammed Ali and Jo Frazier of their time. Sadly, their rivalry came to an abrupt end in 1920 when Joselito was gored to death in the bullring of Talavera de la Reina, aged only 25.

★

'And then there was the elegant Manolete,' interrupted Mr Welles, 'and then my friends Domínguín and Ordóñez. Domínguín was in the ring in Linares when Manolete was fatally gored. He carried the torch from then until Antonio surpassed him.' Mr Welles stood up and gracefully faked a *muleta* pass or two in a rhythmic fashion. 'It is a mysterious ritual. It captivates you. It is an ancient Mediterranean tradition, something to do with the virility of young men and the masculinity of the bulls. Look at those Cretan vases or read the Theseus legend.'

Mr Welles' screenplay, based around the *ferias* that take place Sunday after Sunday all across Spain during the summer months, retraced his Iberian experiences. Years before, in the early fifties, Welles had lived in Madrid and, Hemingway-style, he had followed the *corrida*s and the life that surrounded that ancient dance. He had become close to the two great matadors of that period, Luis Domínguín and Antonio Ordóñez, one the fading maestro, the other the new star with natural raw talent and star appeal. He had followed them to *corrida* after *corrida* around Spain in the bullfighting season as Ordóñez inexorably took everything from Domínguín, including his women, their fates entwined.

In the bullfighting museum in the old bullring in Ronda, black and white photographs of the sleek-haired matadors carousing with Welles gaze down at you like stills from *The Sun Also Rises*.

15

Don Quixote

One morning at breakfast in the Hotel Eden, Mr Welles began to ruminate about *Don Quixote*. I had soldiered through the massive tome by Cervantes while at university. It is strangely intoxicating and very funny. I was fascinated by the idea that Cervantes was an exact contemporary of Shakespeare and actually died on the same day in 1613.

'My Don Quixote and Sancho Panza are exactly and traditionally drawn from Cervantes, but are nonetheless contemporary. What interests me is the *idea* of these dated old virtues. And why they still seem to speak to us when, by all logic, they're so hopelessly irrelevant. That's why I've been obsessed for so long with Don Quixote … he can't *ever* be contemporary – that's really the idea. He never was.'

'Exactly,' I concurred. 'Right from the start, most of his actions are utterly ludicrous but at the same time honourable.'

'He's alive somehow, and he's riding through Spain even now … The anachronism of Don Quixote's knightly armour in what was Cervantes' own modern time doesn't show up very sharply now. I've simply translated the anachronism. My film demonstrates that he and Sancho Panza are eternal.'

'Yes, eternal and global. That human desire to do the right thing despite every setback.'

Mr Welles sat back on the sofa and, taking a new cigar from the box that lay next to him, struck a match and held the flame just below the end of the rolled Cuban tobacco. 'I can't remember the name of the goddamned laboratory where my old footage is. It's ten years since I last looked at it.'

The match flame had now diminished, never having touched the cigar. He shook out the flame and put the disused match into the gigantic hotel ashtray. Sun shone across the curtains of the plush room and all I could hear was his breathing as he lost himself in his own thoughts.

'I'll call Ann Rogers,' I suggested, 'she might know.'

'Good idea, boy.'

So I got through to London and the dependable Mrs Rogers came up with the answer. 'He's got film material all over Europe,' she told me, as I stood there watching him now finally actually light his cigar.

'People say he's running out of countries to work in. He owes money to laboratories in Madrid, Vienna, Paris, London and Rome. They are happy to wait because they have his negatives so at the end of the day they will be paid. If he ever finishes anything.'

Mrs Rogers sounded exasperated with her boss, but she had the name and address of the lab in Rome. I wrote it down on a piece of hotel stationery.

'Hang up, hang up!' he shouted, 'What's she talking about? She's a chatterbox. Has she got the address of the place? Finish.'

Ann Rogers said she'd get off the line, asked me if I was alright, and hung up.

'God Almighty, that woman can talk for England.'

'She had the address.'

'Good, call them and set up an appointment.'

The *Don Quixote* film, all in black and white, lay in a very dusty room in the pre-war film laboratory in the south of Rome near the Basilica of Maria Maggiore. The dilapidated building was halfway down a narrow street. Entering the building, I asked for Ettore Pazzetti. A thin man introduced himself and led me upstairs and into the editing room. Inside were dozens of old film cans with 'Don Quixote' taped on the side. I thanked him and proceeded to identify each can, trying to find the cutting copy, the one I was after. It was hot and filthy work, and pretty soon I was sweating profusely. Tearing off the tape holding the can closed, I pulled out the roll of film and placed it on the editing console.

The dried-up old celluloid began to crackle through the gates of the machine. The imagery I witnessed was extraordinary, as if I were visualising exactly what I had read in Cervantes. Don Quixote himself actually was Don Quixote, Rocinante was as close to the writer's imagination of the old nag as you could imagine. I was mesmerised by Welles' familiar Gothic style of photography – low angles, Dutch angles, wide lenses giving great depth of field so everything in each frame was in focus of the tragic knight wandering hopelessly across the great plains of La Mancha with the overwhelming Spanish sky and fleeting clouds above. The low camera angles accentuated the evidently relentless clear blue sky.

What vision this man had! The footage was mute, but that didn't matter for the moment. The problem was that the splices of the 35mm film had completely dried up now and were threatening to tear open on the sprockets of the editing machine. So I stopped and went down stairs to call Mr Welles.

'How does it look?'

'Tremendous,' I answered. 'The skies are great.'

The static on the line was apparent. Don't forget that making a landline telephone call in the '60s from the south of Rome to the middle of Rome was like making a call from the front line at Monte Cassino back to HQ in Naples during heavy fighting.

'The skies are great?' he bellowed. 'The skies are great! Is that all you can say about all that work I did?'

'No, no,' I spluttered. 'It all looked great, but we need to re-splice the whole thing, otherwise it will fall to bits.'

'And the world would be denied the privilege of seeing Orson Welles' legendary film about Spanish sky? He roared with laughter and I smiled. The phone went dead.

★

'Es imposible hacer una buena pelicula sin una camara que sea como un ojo en el corazon de un poeta.'

So I laboured for two days in that dingy lab which smelled of chemicals and re-spliced the whole film with brand-new Sellotape, which I had to go out and buy in a local stationery shop.

Ettore came into the edit room occasionally while I was working. He had nothing else to do, and I soon got the impression I was probably their first visitor since Carlo Ponti and Sophia Loren had come there to look at some film ten years before. There was a photo of them shaking Ettore's hand in the reception.

Ettore, it turned out, was an Italian colonial. I originally thought he was a colonel in the army, but it was only after many vigorous Italian manual movements that I realised what he was saying. He had been born and raised in Libya where his father had been a shopkeeper. He loved the English, since he had been captured by them during General O'Connor's advances across the Western Desert in 1941. He had been in an artillery regiment and had quickly been rounded up as the English swept by.

'They very kind, very gentleman,' he insisted.

The next day, I drove Mr Welles down to this rundown part of Rome. He rolled out of the car and proceeded into the laboratory, where Ettore greeted him. 'I see you in *Black Rose*. You very good. Also *Third Man*, also *Arkadin*, also *Lady from Shanghai*, also *Jane Eyre*, also *Repulsion*!' Ettore blurted out.

'*Compulsion*,' Welles corrected him, grinning widely. 'Thank you for all that. I am truly flattered. Dorian, can you take us up to the cutting room?'

With that, he followed me up the stairs.

Behind us Ettore went on, 'I love English people. I love you, I love you.' He was getting carried away now.

---

* 'It's impossible to create a good film without a camera that acts like an eye in the heart of a poet.'

'I am not English, *signor*, I am American!' Mr Welles bellowed back down the staircase.

'Would you like to have been an Englishman?' I asked in jest.

'I am in some ways. My family were Anglo-Saxon. I am in love with Shakespeare. What more do you want? Do I qualify?'

As we sat down in the editing room, Mr Welles perched on an editing chair that looked dangerously frail under his enormous weight. 'You know, for some reason, a lot of people, particularly Europeans, think I'm British. Or even Irish.'

'That's a compliment,' I suggested.

'Why you think that?' asked Oja, who had followed us in a taxi.

'Well, we English are respected in many countries. People think of Mr Welles as a gentleman. And the world's perception of a gentleman is an Englishman. David Niven, for example.'

'For God's sake, that is ridiculous!' said Oja, understandably not getting the idea at all. Central Europeans have never grasped the importance of the English because the English are not important to them, so why should they?

'God is an Englishman,' quoted Mr Welles in his best Oxford English. Oja just looked perplexed.

'Let's look at the Spanish man now,' he ordered.

We then ran the film and Mr Welles marked up certain points where he wanted to insert pick-up shots. 'Do you like the skies, Oja?' he asked jokingly.

'Oh, yes, they are truly great. Only you could have shot them like that.'

I smiled but didn't rise to the bait.

So I mustered a crew and some equipment for us to do a few days' shooting on *Don Quixote*. I recced a number of desolate locations outside Rome and Mr Welles chose a disused quarry from my Polaroid pictures. We dressed up a few Italian uncomprehending extras as raggedly clothed *peons*, and shot the footage he had designed.

★

At the sun-baked stone quarry where the crew cars were parked,
I parked under a single cypress tree, which cast a narrow shadow
across my car.

'Do you want me to go closer?'

'No, park here, at the back,' said Mr Welles.

'But I can go closer, if you want,' I replied.

'No, park here, at the back. So we can get away first.'

As we walked over to the set he turned to me, 'Remember that,
Dorian, always park at the back so you can get away first. Tell them
you learnt that from Orson Welles.'

The man Mr Welles had cast to play Quixote had an El Greco-like
long mournful face: he really was 'the man from La Mancha.' He
was a Spanish actor named Francisco Reiguera and he was born
to play the part. The only other part he could have played would
have been Peter the Hermit, the rabble-rousing crusader of the
First Crusade, who reputedly had the jawbone of an ass.

One of those days, I took a call in Rome from him. He asked if
I could give Orson Welles a message. He told me he was the man
who was playing Don Quixote, that it had been ten years since
they had last done any filming and that, if Orson Welles didn't
hurry up, he would be dead before they finished the film.

He was speaking the truth. He did die just a few days after I had
spoken to him.

Mr Welles never revisited that project and the old man, like
Don Quixote before him, died disillusioned.

Quite why Welles never finished these old projects has always
mystified me. Maybe like a painter, he just liked to fiddle with
canvases in no particular order and with no particular game plan
in mind, just daubing a little paint on when the spirit moved him
or, again, like the painter in his studio who had seen greater days
and critical acclaim, he was reluctant to finish anything, fearing
the danger of future failure would be more wounding to his own

self than the harsh words of critics. Whoever wrote that words can never hurt you was a fool. More than that, he could not have been human.

Or maybe Mr Welles just grew bored of projects and ran out of ideas.

★

'Renoir used to say that black was the queen of colours.'

'The painter or the director?' I asked.

'Who do you think?' Mr Welles asked me dismissively.

If he had said he'd just had dinner with Michelangelo, I would have believed him.

'But I like the fact that the first Renoir was an Impressionist painter and his son and grandson were both film-makers. It's like a natural progression of the arts. Film is a new way to paint.'

I thought about that for a moment and realised that he was really a painter of ideas. And his best work was always in black and white.

The memorial to Orson Welles in Ronda. (Author's Collection)

A street sign in Ronda. (Author's Collection)

The spectacularly Gothic Church of Our Lady before Thyn, Prague, sombre in January 1969. (Author's Collection)

The pockmarks of heavy machine-gun-fire on the blackened walls of the National Museum, Wenceslas Square, Prague. (Author's Collection)

NÁMĚSTÍ
JANA PALACHA

1

The short-lived Square of Jan Palach sign. (Author's Collection)

Orson Welles' drawing of me. (Author's Collection)

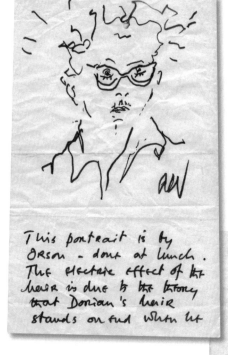

*This portrait is by Orson – done
at lunch. The electric effect of
the hair is due to the theory that
Dorian's hair stands on end
when he…*

*is nervous and is working on the
Moviola!*

*Another interpretation to be
considered is that it is the halo
effect – perhaps theology has
something to do with it!*

Me and Mr Welles,
November 1968.
(Author's Collection)

The habitual cigar.
(Author's Collection)

Charles Gray, Orson Welles and Jonathan Lynn in one of the London skits. (Author's Collection)

Orson Welles and Jeanne Moreau in the deadly dinghy. (Author's Collection)

On location in Venice, September 1969. (Author's Collection)

Ho avuto la fortuna di interpretare
molti di essi, quanto meno in teatro.

Applying make-up, Asolo. (Author's Collection)

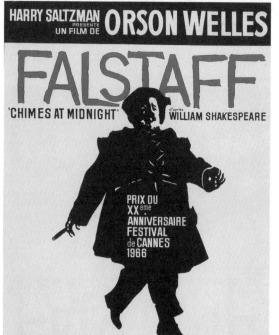

Above: Orson Welles as Shylock, September 1969. (Author's Collection)

Left: Orson Welles, the dainty dancer: the poster for *Chimes at Midnight.* (Author's Collection)

16

A Voice on the Telephone

'Hello, could I speak to Orson Welles?' the voice purred down the line.

'I'm afraid he's not here,' I lied, as Mr Welles gesticulated frantically from the other end of the gigantic suite in the Rome Hilton where we were staying. He had told me just minutes before that he would definitely speak to no one, whoever they were, that morning. He was indisposed or, I suspect, suffering from a hangover from too much cognac the night before.

'I call people when I want to. Those I like I will always call back, so don't worry,' he said.

I could almost hear the breathing at the other end of the line. 'Is that Dorian?' the voice asked.

I nearly dropped the phone and my pulse undoubtedly quickened. 'Yes, it is,' I admitted.

'Orson has told me all about you. He says you are a well-educated young Englishman.'

'Thank you,' I blurted out, as I felt myself blushing to a person at the other end of a telephone line. Mr Welles was by now intrigued as to whom I was talking to and was making enquiring faces at me.

'He tells me you talk of many things and he likes you being around him.' The voice was unmistakable. It was the female voice of the century, with its particular Germanic rolling of the 'r's and its catlike quality.

It was Marlene – Marlene Dietrich.

I had seen her cabaret solo show twice, once in London as a besotted teenager and once in Oxford as a wannabe sophisticated undergraduate. I also had the album of the same show, which was identical to both the performances I'd seen, down to the minutest detail. Her performances were as identical as German cars coming off their factory conveyor belts – just as identical and just as good. Dressed in a glittering silk dress which clung to every inch of her body, she had sashayed through her much-loved songs from 'Lili Marlene' to 'The Boys in the Backroom.'

'Thank you again,' I mumbled. 'Can I tell him who called?'

She chuckled at the end of the line. 'Don't you know who I am?'

'Of course,' I blurted out.

'You have a nice voice,' she teased me.

'So do you, Miss Dietrich,' I managed to respond.

Mr Welles clenched his fists in excitement, realising who it was and seeing my embarrassment.

'Marlene,' she instructed, and I was putty in her hands, 'I will call again tomorrow. Please tell the man that I tried to contact him.'

'Of course I will.'

'It's been fun talking to you.'

I laughed and the phone went dead. I returned it to its cradle and exhaled.

'She's seduced you!' bellowed Mr Welles and roared with laughter. Oja came across the room and pinched my cheeks. 'You're blushing, little Dorian! You're blushing!'

I grinned sheepishly.

'God knows what would happen if you met her.'

'She's an old lady, for goodness sake,' I protested.

'What difference does that make?' announced Mr Welles, 'Marlene will ring again tomorrow and for sure you are going to answer the phone.'

And so it went on for quite a few days, my love affair with Marlene Dietrich via the telephone. On the first day she mischievously started off with a statement. 'Orson has a big complex about his nose.'

'Really?' I responded.

'Yes, he has. Have you ever thought about it? He has a beautiful little nose. But it's a baby nose, small and turned up at the end.'

Mr Welles was staring at me and trying to work out what La Dietrich was saying to me. He loved the whole game. I pretended to look serious and stared straight back at his baby nose.

'A baby nose, *sans question*,' she purred on. 'Just think of it, in most of his movies he's changed it, *Touch of Evil*, *A Man for all Seasons*, *Lady from Shanghai*, and so on and so on. He's never comfortable with his own nose. Widiculous!' she pronounced, in her Germanic voice.

Come to think of it, she was dead right. The only person I could think of who had put on an equal number of false noses was Laurence Olivier, who looked equally bad. I never understand why they bothered. We all knew who it was playing the part and it only distracted us watching the widiculous noses, churned out film after film. Take them all away and we could concentrate on the actor, accept him as a performer and move on to enjoying his performance. What can you say? Marlene was dead right, as she was about a lot of things.

The next call was started with the usual silence along the line from Paris. I knew it would be her. This time she began to sing. 'You're the cweam in my coffee, you're the … I can't remember the words. Anyway, you are literally the cweam in my morning coffee which I'm enjoying right now. You know I sang that song at my first audition for *The Blue Angel*. I was hopeless, or at least the pianist was. I ended up singing a German song I knew much better.'

The next day she again started to sing. This time, 'Falling in Love Again, what am I to do?'

'I saw you sing that twice in my life. Once in London as a child with my mother and then more recently at Oxford.'

'Well then, you are a fan,' she purred flirtatiously.

'Yes, I am,' I blushed again. This was pathetic. I was putty in the hands of a septuagenarian ringing from Paris and I was in Rome. It was telephone seduction, pure and simple.

Another morning she confided in me a little story which, out of loyalty, I never repeated to Mr Welles. She told me that he never fancied blonde women and was much more taken by the Latin look. As she told me, I realised she was right – Dolores Del Rio, Rita Hayworth, Lea Padovani, Paola Mori, and now Oja, these were the women of his life.

'For *Touch of Evil* he put me in a dark wig which completely changed everything. Before that we had been good friends. We still are, despite the fact that he won't take my calls at the moment! I can live with that. So when he first saw me in the wig he became a different man. I could see lust in his eyes. I'm serious. Lust, pure and simple.' She laughed her breathy laugh. 'For the rest of the movie I had to lock my dressing room. I was terrified he might even beat the door down! Dear sweet Orson, I adore him, you know. And I suspect he's drawn you into his spider's web!'

'A little,' I confessed, 'But I'm loving it.'

'Of course, enjoy him while you may. He is a feast of a human being. He is some kind of a man.'

The line between us fell silent, save for the electrical static as I savoured those words.

'I have to stop now,' she purred, 'I have things to do. *Auf wiedersehen. À bientôt.* Goodbye. *Adios.*'

The phone went dead, and as I hung up I reflected on this remarkable woman whose presence had dominated my childhood and adolescence, not just with her films and her cabaret performances exuding her enormous personality but for her bravery in the war years to stand against Nazi Germany, her homeland, and to denounce as pretenders those evil men who had defiled her beloved country.

Perhaps the best memory for me of this great woman was her final scene in *Touch of Evil* with her line, 'He was some kind of a man.' It was as though she was talking about Mr Welles. She probably was.

And her final word to me had been '*Adios*,' just like her final word in the movie as she walked away.

Marlene Dietrich was a phenomenon. Beautiful, in the true sense of the word, poised, classy, distant, always alluring yet tangible, vulnerable, sexy and intimate, with that voice with its Teutonic giveaways that could make your blood run cold or your temperature rise. She was the personification of a star: alluring yet distant, intimate yet unavailable, and all the time elegant and classy. Her beauty and haughtiness were embellished by her open opposition to those grubby men that ruled Germany after she had left her mother country. She despised them, she had contempt for them, and she has never been applauded enough for her brave stand against them, and it broke her heart when she knew that this brought her into direct opposition to her mother country.

So, as young men from her country fought and died as patriots, she supported their opponents in a very real way and sang them the songs that, in another time, she would have sung for her own people. Like Mr Welles, she was one of a kind. A one-off. In my book, in the pantheon of gods and goddesses of the twentieth century, she will always stand alongside Mr Welles.

Emerging from Weimar Berlin, she first seduced the world with her captivating performance in *The Blue Angel* as a femme fatale, where she first performed her legendary 'Falling in Love Again,' directed by Josef von Sternberg. From those images *Cabaret* was to appear decades later, based on Christopher Isherwood's experiences in Berlin at that time.

Hollywood then called, and her world fame ensued. Sternberg, who already with a reputation in Hollywood, had returned to Germany specifically to direct *The Blue Angel*. He returned to the US with her, and together they made six more pictures with Hollywood for Paramount. Their plan was to create their own German 'ice queen' to combat Metro Goldwyn's Swedish Greta Garbo.

17/

BREAKING BREAD

Lunch on the Piazza Navona, this time at the Panzirone. We wisely Wellesian-select an indoor table to:

1 stay out of the sun, which is too hot
2 not be recognised by roaming paparazzi or tourists.

Remember, Mr Welles is probably one of the most recognisable people of the twentieth century. And it's not just the face, it's the body too.

Spaghetti alla Vongole, then *Aragosta alla Termidoro*. He's on a lobster diet, but this is one of the most spectacularly rich dishes I've ever encountered:

> It was in the Revolutionary calendar of Thermidor that the monstrous Robespierre was overthrown. I'll eat to that step towards democracy. It's a human tragedy that revolutions started with good intentions invariably end up with some psychopath like Robespierre trying to hijack them. In fact, it is almost an inevitable result. In America, thank God, our revolutionaries were rational and democratic men.

We talk of characters. Oliver Reed:

> We made *I'll Never Forget What's his Name*. He has a presence, a powerful presence. Almost menacing. If he doesn't let drink

destroy him, he could become a major star. He is formidable. I like him. He's Carol's nephew, you know.

Gary Cooper:

A lovely man. And so handsome. He was a true friend of mine. I didn't think much of him as an actor. Remember I was a man of the theatre. He never projected, just was himself, but, boy, what a presence. I remember once watching him at work. The director took just three takes. I thought there was nothing there. When I saw the rushes I realised how wrong I was. He was a star.

Kenneth Tynan:

Dear Ken, he has a self-destruct button. Apparently at Oxford he was Oscar Wilde, Aubrey Beardsley and Swinburne all rolled into one. He is truly debauched and you can't say that about many people. He told me he's a sadomasochist with great enthusiasm, for God's sake! What was I supposed to say? Good for you? He wrote his first book and asked me to write the foreword. He told me that if I didn't they wouldn't publish the book.

So I did.

He's a master of words, a fascinating character straight out of the nineteenth century.

The notion of Kenneth Tynan, one of my literary heroes, vigorously spanking women completely threw me. I was an innocent. To some extent, Mr Welles was the same, in that he always struck me as a red-blooded heterosexual with normal, or what I perceived as normal, appetites.

Mr Welles continued, 'Tell me, Dorian. Was Oxford like that when you were there?'

'There is a certain sensuality, a softness about Oxford which doesn't exist in Cambridge. Oxford is Oscar Wilde and Cambridge is Oliver Cromwell; Oxford is Shelley and Cambridge is Milton.'

'And Shakespeare and Dickens went nowhere near either place,' he breathed, pleased with his interjection.

I droned on. 'It's a ridiculous comparison, but there is something epicurean about Oxford and something puritanical about Cambridge. Oxford is more laissez-faire, more enquiring and less accepting. Cambridge is more disciplined, more mathematical, more conservative. The stone in Oxford is warm sandstone; in Cambridge it is cold, white Portland stone. Oxford is in the soft hills of Oxfordshire; Cambridge is on the windswept fens of East Anglia, and when the east wind blows it comes out of Central Russia.'

'My goodness, you're getting poetic Dorian.'

'But there is some truth is my generalisations,' I insisted.

Mr Welles listened on a subject he knew little about. 'So I would have been a Cambridge man since I had that scholarship to Harvard?'

'Yes, I suppose,' I answered, 'but you are clearly an Oxford character in the way you live your life.'

Mr Welles cogitated a little as he chewed his lobster. 'I suspect you might be right, Dorian.'

He paused and took a long draft from his glass of Barolo. 'And where was Byron?' He had me. He always had to be right. He always had to have the last word.

'Cambridge,' I acknowledged, 'and he, of all people, should have been to Oxford. Probably Christ Church or Magdalen.'

'Since I'm not one of you Englishmen, it's all irrelevant.'

'Chaplin?' I asked.

'Another of the monsters. An Englishman, of course. How could he not be with his success? He was without doubt the most famous man in the world. But his sex drive was dangerously screwed. It always amuses me that Nabokov wrote *Lolita* when he lived next door to Chaplin in Switzerland. Coincidence?'

Piazza Navona and Steve McQueen

'Bernini is a much-underestimated man. People talk about Leonardo and Michelangelo and Rafael – I'm talking about people in general not art experts – and they never mention Bernini. Yet much of the Rome we live in is the vision of Bernini. That magnificent oval colonnade leading up to St Peter's: that's his creation.'

We were sitting in the Ristorante Tre Scalini in the Piazza Navona and gazing at the Fontana dei Quattro Fiumi, the centre-piece of that great oval space, originally the Circus of Domitian.

'The obelisk was brought to Rome from Egypt by Caracalla and …' I added.

'Come on, Dorian, this is getting boring, let's go and catch a movie,' Oja interrupted laughingly. 'Orson will not be impressed with your knowledge of Classical Rome.'

That was an abrupt put-down, but I guess endless afternoons sitting in luxury hotel suites waiting for Mr Welles to return from working with me might have got a little tedious. I always scented a frisson of jealousy of his interest in me. But that's how it was.

Mr Welles sucked vigorously on his cigar like a contented baby. I waited for his reaction and tried to catch his eye. 'I thought you, as a sculptress, would admire the work of Bernini?' he teased.

'Too florid and elaborate for me, too baroque. A movie would be more fun.'

'Why not,' he breathed out, his words accompanied by the smoke of his exhalation, that rich-smelling smoke of burning Cuban tobacco leaves rolled between the perspiring thighs of Cuban girls.

I am getting carried away here and must return to the subject in hand. Picture three people, a 59-year-old, hugely overweight American film director, a slim-built sculptress in her mid-thirties from Yugoslavia, and a callow youth of 24, an Englishman. Or an English boy, depending on how you look at it.

Oja whooped with delight and quickly asked a waiter for a newspaper so we could look up a film. Remember, this was still that prehistoric time when nobody had mobile phones, no computers, let alone phones that were connected to the World Wide Web. What the hell was that?

A filthy old Roman paper was produced and we scanned through it. In the big cinemas there were a number of Italian movies on like Fellini's *Satyricon*, but at the Cinema Americano, a fleapit in Trastevere, *Bullitt*, starring Steve McQueen, was still showing.

None of us had any idea of what it was about, but we arrived at the movie theatre in the middle of the afternoon and I bought three tickets at the back and on the aisle. Now cinema seats in those days were compact, to put it mildly, and narrow and with little leg room – the same as the Royal Opera House at Covent Garden in London, but that's another story and I'm not talking about opera or ballet right now.

★

'The Opera is a much-overestimated sport, indulged in by people with little love of music or drama, more interested in showing off their wealth to people of their own kind, who cannot afford to buy great paintings, or the intellect to tolerate great theatre or the emotional depth or patience to sit through a Beethoven symphony. They are philistines disguising themselves as aesthetes. Opera is

mystery to me: a combination of incredibly moving and melodic arias strung together by weak storylines performed by fat people. I should talk!

'Balletomanes, on the other hand, are the real deal. To a restricted repertoire of classical ballet, restricted by the sheer lack of ballets choreographed to classical music pieces, they attend again and again and frantically applaud the muscular panegyrics of, very often, mediocre talents.

'When the great ballet dancers, male or female, do perform to their utmost, there are few arts which come close to their emotional heights.

Did you know the Bolshoi Ballet just means Big Ballet? Sounds not so dramatic!'

Anyway, in the dim light at the back of the Cinema America, Mr Welles shooed me into the first seat, Oja next to me, and then he took his place on the outside seat on the aisle. As he placed his enormous weight on the miniscule seat it creaked ominously, but he stuck out his legs into the aisle, which clearly took some of his weight. He stretched his arm round Oja and wedged himself into position. It was a tour de force of agility, ingenuity and raw courage, which is what you would expect from the maestro.

Another thing is that, in those days, smoking was allowed in cinemas. In fact, ashtrays were often built into the seating. People also smoked on fuel-laden aircraft. Can you imagine? So, with his arm around Oja, he reached into his top pocket and extricated his next cigar and placed it in his mouth. Then with his right hand he deftly pulled out his matches and one-handedly managed to light it.

For the next two hours he held this position, and it was worth it, as we were transported to the streets of San Francisco and experienced probably the best film car chase ever made at that point in time in cinema history. (If it's car chases that turn you on.)

As we walked back through the Piazza di Santa Maria towards the Tiber, Mr Welles bought some flowers from a flower-seller and presented them to Oja. She giggled happily. He said little about the film, which I think had bored him. In truth, he wasn't really interested in looking at other people's films. The notion that a film-maker has to be well-versed in film history is a myth. Very often, film buffs are not film-makers, just as literary critics and literary agents are, most times, not writers.

'He's got a presence about him,' said Mr Welles, talking about Steve McQueen. 'He's laid back, but at the same time he has the ability to exude a certain menace. He means it. The only other guy I can think of in that league is Lee Marvin, who can do the threat of impending violence like no actor I know.'

'Don't you think his walk in his suede loafers was a little camp?' asked Oja mischievously.

Mr Welles roared with laughter. 'McQueen, camp? Well, I never thought of that!'

Bullitt was the only film I ever watched in its entirety with Mr Welles and I'm not sure it was exactly his cup of tea. Nevertheless, I suspect he enjoyed it, though he wouldn't admit it, symbolising as it did the simplicity of what Hollywood does best, which is to entertain in a very basic manner and nothing more. No Mozarts here, nor Raphaels, nor Shakespeares either, that's for sure.

As I walked back to my hotel, having dropped off Oja and Mr Welles, I wondered how Steve McQueen would stack up in history against Gian Lorenzo Bernini.

19

Bedroom Gymnastics

'You do sex with Mr Orson?'

The question was followed with a classic limp-wristed wave. 'You like sex with Mr Orson?'

The person persisted. This second question was followed by a shrill laugh. I smiled back, which merely encouraged more questions.

'*Quanto*? How much he pay you?'

'Not a lot,' I smiled back.

'He pay you each time? How you do it with him? He very big, you very small.'

The person behind the voice was a young man called Romolo, a character in the narrow street where I lived. He was a hairdresser and spent much of his day leaning on his salon doorway and smoking the mild cigarettes of choice, Muratti.

I was changing the tyre of my Mini, which had a slow puncture. As I laboured away in the heat and the noise of the street, I was subjected to this barrage of questions. Placing a car jack on the optimum flat surface in a cobbled street probably as old as Rome itself is a difficult exercise. Brutus and Cassius had probably driven their chariots along this very street. As I struggled with the piece of heavy metal, I understood what a deadly weapon it could be, used in countless murders since its first invention. Romolo, fortunately for him, was blissfully unaware of the murderous thoughts stirred up by my Irish temper. Unfortunately, he had often seen me in local tavernas with Mr Welles and had even once seen me drive by in my car with Mr Welles as the passenger. He knew I was Mr Welles' errand boy and drew his own lecherous conclusions.

Romolo continued with his teasing, which appeared to amuse him more than me. He was merely voicing the smutty thoughts of many of Rome's *tifosi*, who read the local rags. The fact that a pretty young man might be an object of desire for an ageing Hollywood star was certainly not beyond the realms of possibility, but there it remained, in the realms of possibility and nowhere else. Rock Hudson had not yet been outed.

As to the gymnastics of Mr Welles in the erotic area, I merely imagined that logic took over and practicality took the driving seat. For Mr Welles was, to my certain knowledge, a red-blooded heterosexual with a very impressive CV by any standards. Italy, the country that had produced Casanova and where the philandering male was admired perhaps more than anywhere else in the world, should have known that better than anyone.

His CV was surely a thing of wonder to most men: Geraldine Fitzgerald, Dolores Del Rio, Rita Hayworth, Jennifer Jones, Marlene Dietrich, Eartha Kitt, Paola Mori and now Olga Palinkas. If ever there was a list of well-bred, intelligent, kind and beautiful women, this was it. But there again, we are dealing with not just a mountain of a man but a man with a mountainous mind and matching energy, charm, imagination, and charisma beyond the reach of mere mortals.

To go back to the subject of how Mr Welles actually managed to indulge in sexual relations – that was not really of interest to me and, anyway, I'm sure he managed in some way or other, using his imagination, his experience, his cunning and his knowledge of the laws of physics. Beyond that I will keep my peace. Suffice it to say that Mr Welles was an aficionado of women, as much as he was of wine, food, cigars, history, politics and most other subjects known to man.

★

One day in jest, I advanced on him with a dagger, dressed in my costume for The Merchant of Venice. Without a word, he grabbed a sword and struck the dagger out of my hand.

'Wow!' *I gasped.*

Mr Welles turned away, threw his sword to the marble floor and growled, 'I was the sabre champion of southern California, 1947, so beware, young man.'

Romolo finished his cigarette, squashed it under his Gucci loafer, and turned to go back into his salon.

I had finished changing my tyre.

'You wouldn't do that if you smoked an expensive cigar!' I called after him.

'Cigars are for men. I am a girl, Mr Doriano!' Romolo cackled, as he disappeared back to his trade when a brassy Roman lady of the night arrived for her hairdo.

'Exactly,' I said, 'Only real men smoke cigars.'

And Mr Welles was a real man.

20

THIRTEEN IS NOT A LUCKY NUMBER

In July Mr Welles was contracted to appear in a bizarre movie called *Thirteen Chairs*, based on a Russian surrealist story. It was an Anglo-Italian co-production featuring Orson Welles, Vittorio Gassman, Vittorio de Sica, Tim Brooke-Taylor (the English comedian), Terry Thomas and Sharon Tate. What an extraordinary cast. Even the process of typing it out astonishes me, as I read the names and try to think of some connection between them. There is none, they are just characters whom the hero meets in his search to find the chairs, one of which holds the treasure. Hence the word 'surrealist.' Suffice it to say, the end result was truly awful.

Mr Welles' scenes were to be shot in an old Roman theatre built onto a Renaissance garden owned by a member of the Roman Black Aristocracy, the Colonnas, Orsinis or Aldobrandinis. These so-called Black Aristocrats were the temporal princes of the Roman Catholic Church, with bloodlines running back directly to the early Middle Ages.

The significance of this is that Mr Welles was being pursued by Alexander Paal, a Hungarian producer who was trying to serve a writ on him for walking out after one day's shooting of a Karen Blixen story set in Budapest. 'When I got there I quickly realised the whole thing was a scam.'

'The Hungarians are unquestionably,' Mr Welles told me, by way of explanation, 'the best linguists and the most devious businessmen in Europe. He was never going to pay me. Never trust a Hungarian.

'There is a thing about downtrodden nations. Since they cannot control you or command you, they trick you. They consider that part of their human rights. In film production it is a regular practice: they quote a low price to get you to start the production in their country or their studio, then they hike the price and throw their arms up in the air as if it is a surprise.'

This apparently devious Hungarian would lurk outside the theatre every day, having got wind of the fact that Mr Welles would have to attend there. So I, in my deadly multi-purpose Mini, was instructed by Mr Welles to find a secret way of getting him to the theatre location they were shooting in. I scouted the area and found another way into the theatre by going round to the main gate of the palazzo and explaining to the head gardener that no less a person than Orson Welles needed private access for the filming.

So, each morning we would drive through Renaissance stone gates opened by the gardener, for a considerable contribution, into this rather beautiful and faded formal Italian garden, to arrive at a back entrance to the theatre. I would then exit the theatre by the main entrance and wait while Mr Welles did his shooting. For some days, I brought him bottles of cognac, which he would imbibe between takes while sweating profusely. The Hungarian producer fairly soon cottoned onto the fact that I was Mr Welles' sidekick and proceeded to harass me with questions, of course in fluent English, as to 'the American bastard's' whereabouts.

It was on one of these days that I had lunch at a little Italian (what else would it be in Rome?) restaurant across the street from the location with the all-American starlet Sharon Tate, newly married to Roman Polanski. She was all you would imagine – clean-cut, healthy-skinned, Californian good looks, with big eyes and a great set of teeth, a thing which the English always admire in Americans. And she was heavily pregnant.

'I only took this film so I could tell my grandchildren that I'd once worked with Orson Welles. I thought at one point I wouldn't be able to because of my condition, look at me!' she told me. 'I'm just so thrilled to meet him. What a gentleman. And that voice. Wow! It blew me away.' Her character matched her looks, all open, unbridled enthusiasm.

I ordered pasta for us in my workable Italian. As the waiter turned away, she called after him, '*E un bicchiere di acqua minerale per me, per favore.*'

I was impressed. 'You speak Italian, as well? That's great!'

'No, just a few words. My father was in the service and we were stationed in Verona and I went to school for a time in Vicenza.'

I twisted my fork through my spaghetti and expertly took a mouthful.

'Roman speaks lots of languages,' she continued, 'French, English and Polish of course. He's so intelligent.'

She had met Roman Polanski when she was cast in *The Fearless Vampire Killers*, an unfortunate title in the light of later events, for Martin Ransohoff's Filmways, who had produced *The Cincinnati Kid*, *The Sandpiper*, with Burton and Taylor, and a number of other successful films.

I continued to tuck into my pasta as did she. She ate voraciously. 'I'm sorry, I'm eating like a horse these days!'

'No problem, looks natural to me,' I mumbled, stunned by the sheer natural beauty of the female sitting in front of me and astonished by her enchanting directness.

That afternoon she was taking a flight out of Rome to London. As she left, she kissed me politely on the cheek and said, 'You talk just like Roman. All that enthusiasm. All that burning ambition.'

I stepped back and opened the door of her limousine and watched as she sped away. My heart was beating faster than it normally does. A week later, hers was not beating at all, nor was that of the baby inside her.

21

LONDON

Some few days after this, we upped sticks to London, or 'Swinging London,' as it was latterly labelled. The place where I had come from was now full of accessible rock stars, footballers with extremely short shorts and very long hair, available marijuana, flared trousers, big hairstyles for boys, and girls as skinny as Twiggy often with boys' short haircuts.

Mr Welles had predictably planned to shoot the 'England' part of a CBS special there, produced by the ageing Carter de Haven, entitled *The Many Faces of Orson Welles*.

Also his wife and daughter lived there.

So, I discovered, not only was his artistic and financial life complicated, but also his private life. He had one wife in London and another in Europe. In fact, Mr Welles had married in London, which he only revealed to me in an aside as we walked down the King's Road, Chelsea, past Chelsea Town Hall. 'I got married in there to my beautiful wife,' he said wistfully.

Carter de Haven had worked as an assistant director on *The Caine Mutiny* and *Days of Wine and Roses*. Over lunch at Wheelers on Old Compton Street, he and Mr Welles talked about Chaplin, who had worked with his father on *Modern Times* and *The Great Dictator*.

'You have to remember he was the most famous man in the world. He even said he was more famous than Jesus Christ. And Lenin said he was the only man he wanted to meet. He was a complete monster on set apparently. Shooting thousands of feet of film at a very high ratio and shouting at anyone who suggested they move on. My father always told me in confidence that *The Great Dictator* was less a political satire than a sort of homage to Hitler. Hitler watched the film twice.'

'They could have been twins!' roared Mr Welles. 'Of course, he was a goddamned psychopath. I know because I worked with him on *Verdoux*.'

'I had forgotten that you wrote *Monsieur Verdoux*,' said de Haven.

'He continually thought he was "improving" my script and made changes on set when I wasn't there, then told me about it afterwards. And you know what? He missed one particular idea which I thought would be great. In the story, Verdoux is a teetotaller, a complete teetotaller. In the end scene, which I wrote, I had him approach the scaffold and be offered a little cognac. My idea was that he would accept it and drink it then, in his expression, like it and regret he hadn't been a drinker all his life!' Mr Welles roared with laughter.

'Great,' said de Haven.

'But he never put it in,' sighed Mr Welles. He took a mouthful of the Barolo we were drinking, then another. 'You know his next-door neighbour in Switzerland was Nabokov?'

'I never realised,' replied de Haven.

'I think Nabokov got his idea for *Lolita* from watching Chaplin. He would have made a better Humbert Humbert than James Mason. He was the real thing.'

'They are remarkable, those writers who write in more than one language. Nabokov was one, and of course, Joseph Conrad. I always wanted to make *Heart of Darkness*, would make a great movie.'

★

On 10 August, I was walking up St James's Street just off Piccadilly to meet Mr Welles at Brown's Hotel in Mayfair. A few doors up were the offices of John Murray, the publishers, in whose first-floor drawing room old John Murray himself, the confidant and friend of Byron, had cast the great poet's potentially hugely valuable diaries into the fire, page by scandalous page.

On the other side of the street stood a darkened and disused doorway where, a year earlier, I had met another renegade director, Michael Powell. Mistakenly thinking that because I lived in Switzerland I was a source of private film funding, he had talked to me enthusiastically about his new project *The Tempest*, with James Mason to play Prospero.

Filled with these unconnected thoughts, I passed a newspaper stand blaring the headlines 'Sharon Tate Murdered.'

I was stunned.

On her way back to Los Angeles via London, she had been interviewed. 'My whole life has been decided by fate. I think something more powerful than we are decides our fates for us. I know one thing – I've never planned anything that ever happened to me.'

Reading the gruesome details made it even worse, when I conjured up images of what had happened to her next to the images I still had of my lunch with that young woman. Here is not the place to talk about Sharon Tate's ghastly last moments as, covered in blood from multiple hate-filled stab wounds, she pleaded for her unborn baby's life to be saved, but was met with blank unfeeling eyes before her blood-soaked body slipped lifeless to the floor. The thought of a healthy and lively human transforming to a bloody carcass of flesh is an image that haunts me to this day. Charles Manson certainly ended the innocence of flower power and long hair.

For the Carter de Haven CBS production, we shot a number of London and English clichés for an American audience:

Mr Welles as a Covent Garden flower-seller à la Nell Gwyn, jokes with London policemen, London telephone boxes, funny walks with Tim Brooke-Taylor in Carnaby Street.

Mr Welles as an English aristocrat at the gates of his country pile with his twit of an heir, Morris dancing at Ham House, a beautiful Queen Anne-style stately home on the banks of the River Thames at

Richmond, where rich men in the 1800s built themselves summer-houses to escape the fetid city (a sort of late-seventeenth-century Hamptons). To get a better angle Mr Welles asked for the camera to be placed on the roof of the camera van we had hired. He then proceeded to daintily clamber up onto the roof of the said van. He was more agile than you would expect, but science could not be overruled and he created an enormous dent in the roof.

We performed sketches devised by Mr Welles with the Goodies. (*The Goodies* was a popular TV show at the time, featuring Tim Brooke-Taylor, Bill Oddie and Graham Garden, a sort of post-Beatles pre-Monty Python anarchic show.)

That evening, we all went out to dinner and I drank too much. I was so hungover early on the Sunday morning that I presented the clapperboard to the camera backwards. Mr Welles roared, half-exasperated, half-amused. The sheer volume of his voice echoed up and down the rather narrow Soho street, causing an irate hooker to shout down from an upstairs window to tell everyone to shut up. It was like a scene out of the back streets of Naples.

After filming another cliché scene with Tim Brooke-Taylor as a particularly moronic London policeman, we repaired to the Hilton on Hyde Park for breakfast. I was feeling too ill to eat, but couldn't help noticing Mr Welles ordering a steak while a ballet dancer (one of the extras) had Rice Krispies. When I asked him why he didn't order more, he replied, 'As a dancer, I have to keep myself in shape.' He then glanced disapprovingly up the table at Mr Welles, 'Unlike some other people in show business I could mention.'

After breakfast, we went back to Soho and Tim Brooke-Taylor did a 'silly walk' in Carnaby Street. The ballet dancer couldn't see the joke of the mincing walk.

Then we all went to lunch at Isow's, that famous Jewish restaurant, long since closed down, in Brewer Street. It was London's answer to Sardi's in New York, with walls covered in signed photographs of bad actors, corrupt politicians and boxers. The seating was plush, red plastic chairs with celebrity names embossed on the back. There was, of course, a photograph of Mr Welles. He glanced at it and I asked him when it was taken.

'Just when Larry Olivier had made my life hell over my production of Ionesco's *Rhinoceros* and I had walked out! My God, he could be such a stickler for detail. He was so great in some of his performances and such an old ham in many others. Like all us thespians! You're really only as good as your material. You know, he wasn't that bright and he had that strange empty quality about him which many great actors have. It's as if the character they play is inserted into them. No character to play, not much there.'

'But you are not in that category.'

'Well, am I a great actor or just a good one – sometimes?'

★

'What did you study at university, Dorian?'

'Theology, Mr Welles.'

'Seriously?'

'Yes, I did. It was great. Biblical studies of course, but also a fair bit of ancient history and the Reformation.' There was a pause, then I asked him, 'What would you have studied? History?'

'No, certainly not. Most of history is lies written down by the winners.' He puffed again on a newly ignited cigar. Smoke filled the air between us.

'And your history?' I asked.

'Much myth.'

I liked that, through the smoky silence between us. He was both a myth and a man.

'Anthropology. That would interest me. The origins of man. How we are all connected. Where we all come from. Darwin and all that.' He paused again in thought. 'You know I had a scholarship to Harvard. After my father died, Roger Hill wanted me to stay on at school and it was he who secured the university connection. But I didn't want to be so formally educated. I wanted to educate myself, which I have done. So, I ran away.'

★

One afternoon, I was having tea with Mr Welles at Brown's Hotel in London. He told me he liked it because it was centrally located and a little cheaper than some of the alternatives. 'What's good enough for Oscar Wilde and Bram Stoker is good enough for me.'

Come to think of it, Mr Welles had much in common with the legendary Wilde – he was instantly recognisable in the street, he had razor-sharp wit and repartee, he was an artistic all-rounder, he was a great conversationalist, he knew or had known anybody you cared to mention, and he was somewhat of an outcast, an outsider in the circles in which he mixed. He was a stranger in his own house, peopled as it was by men of lesser stature. I prayed he would not suffer Oscar's sad fate.

As I got up to attract the attention of a sleepy waiter, I was suddenly approached by an American former contemporary of mine at the gloriously titled London School of Film Technique. He had hardly given me the time of day while there, but now it was a different matter. Clearly, he was suitably impressed and took me aside.

'So you really are working for Orson Welles?' he spluttered. 'That must be great. But I guess he's not what he was. What's he really done since *Citizen Kane*?'

This was typical film school talk where *Citizen Kane* was worshipped but any subsequent films by Welles were dismissed as disappointing. Well, I beg to differ and, in any event, if he had just made *Citizen Kane* and nothing else he would still be a giant of the cinema. And what about his performance as Clarence Darrow in *Repulsion*, or as Falstaff? All these thoughts raced through my mind before I dismissed my film school acquaintance with a scathing reply. 'A few things,' I murmured and turned on my heel.

I sat down again as the fresh pot of tea was delivered, comfortable at the metaphorical foot of the maestro, realising sadly that he would always be fated to be judged by that millstone of a work of art. Much of his other work stands him head and shoulders above most film-makers I can think of, but for some reason, any description of him was always prefaced with a sigh, a sneer, or a rolling of the eyes, as if he had failed. Failed at what?

Some few years later, when I was working with more contemporarily fashionable directors like Ridley Scott and Hugh Hudson on commercials, whenever his name was mentioned it was as if he somehow hadn't 'made it.' Worst of all, nobody was that interested. It was as if he came from another time.

It was hard not to be impressed by Mr Welles. Even if you had no idea who he was, you couldn't fail to be awed by his sheer physical presence and the volume and timbre of his voice. And if you got closer you would be struck by his wit, his intellect and his sheer breadth of knowledge and command of languages.

★

'My father took me to China when I was just a boy.'

'Mine took me all over Europe before I was a teenager.'

'But I never really had the father-son thing. He was always away travelling. It was my mother who awoke my interest in the arts and, of course, Roger Hill. She was a concert-level pianist.'

'What did you inherit from them?'

'No money, that's for sure! Seriously, he taught me to seize opportunity when it came along. She taught me that any art form, if practised, was a lot of hard work.'

'Do you feel you never had a father really?'

'No, I did have that elusive man as my father, and then I had Dr Bernstein, my mother's friend, as my sort of godfather. If I needed money I went to him, until I realised he was taking my inheritance! What I learnt from my mother was to chance things, to challenge people, and to not be afraid to show them what I could do. It's worked so far, but boy, sometimes, it seems as though I am constantly walking uphill.

And when I get paid money, it always seems too late or even too early. The problem with this business unlike other art forms is you need big bucks to do anything. You need an army to make a film, whereas a painter just needs a canvas and some paint. Most of these actors and their agents are so goddam greedy, though they pretend not to be. When did you last see a talk show host ask an actor what he got paid for his last picture? Occasionally a few of them have done me favours, but it's rare. So, I make promises regarding payment I can't keep, chasing my dreams.

I often wonder how many of these people would be in the business if there wasn't so much money floating around. Theatre people were much less driven by the dollar and in general were much nicer. Hell, you have to be more disciplined in the theatre, you have to learn your lines!

I think of myself as a man of the theatre born into the time of the cinema, or even the time of TV.'

★

He really was a Renaissance man, exuding power (natural to him), perception and artistry. In that good directors should really be the ringmaster at the circus, Mr Welles had these qualities in abundance, both with his own innate skills, his flair for orchestrating others' abilities and his ability to spot the talents of others. The creative urge was always burning inside him, driving him forward with endless changing ideas and projects. He might perhaps have thrived better these days, with the newfound power of the independent producers with whom he could have made endless idiosyncratic films for a faithful audience, rather in the way that Woody Allen or Merchant Ivory have operated. Sadly, he straddled the time when the power of the great Hollywood studios, though fading, was still in position, but the independent production scene had not yet really established itself.

22

A New York Dandy

The suave Harvard-educated Arnold Weissberger was a dandy. He dressed liked a gentleman: always a bow tie and always the signature white carnation in his buttonhole. Today he was in a pin-striped suit and a beautiful pair of handmade shoes, probably from Lobbs of London. Milton Goldman, his partner and lover for all his adult life, was at his side, looking suitably content. Like a happy pumpkin, he was redder in face than Arnold but equally dapper.

Relationships and marriages in those days were accepted as facts. Nobody discussed or analysed them, they just accepted them and got on with it. It is only in recent years that this obsession with identifying people by their sexual proclivities has, for some reason, become the fashion. People have been behaving like this for thousands of years, and why not? What people do behind closed doors is their own business and good luck to them.

Mr Welles had first been introduced to Arnold Weissberger by his sister, who had been working with the youthful Welles ever since he came to Broadway and during those early days with John Houseman. Weissberger was a young, thrusting lawyer and the 20-year-old Welles was carving himself a reputation on Broadway.

They greeted us enthusiastically as we entered the restaurant on the Piazza Navona. A sophisticated-looking camera lay on the white tablecloth in front of him and, as the meal progressed, he proceeded to grab it from time to time and snap portraits of us at the table. Mr Welles didn't seem to object. He explained jocularly, 'He's not just a hard-assed lawyer, he's also a great photographer.'

I thought he was joking, until I discovered later that Weissberger did indeed conduct both careers successfully in parallel. His main claim to success was that he represented many of the old Hollywood players. Igor Stravinsky, Lauren Bacall, Laurence Oliver, David O. Selznick, and of course, Orson Welles, were all looked after by him. But, unlike many agents and lawyers of the famous, he was a star in his own right, throwing legendary parties in Manhattan.

'Did you know Arnold and Milton throw A-list parties and B-list parties?' guffawed Mr Welles.

Milton just chuckled, before Arnold responded, 'And you, Orson, little as you pay me, will always be on our A list!'

★

'Arnold is so paranoid about Milton looking at other men that he only employs elderly male waiters at his parties rather than dashing young studs,' joked Mr Welles as he quaffed his glass of wine.

'That's a little sad,' said Oja kindly, smiling.

Their relationship seemed rock-solid, I thought to myself. On the face of it, it was a bit of a cliché – the classic beautiful young actress with the ageing movie director – but far from it. Mr Welles and Oja had a connection physically and artistically. They wanted the same things and understood each other well. She admired him and he admired her.

★

As lunch progressed, Arnold told us that he had visited his old friend Alicia Markova while in England. 'One of the great Russian ballerinas,' I clumsily mumbled.

'Markova was not Russian! She was English, by the name of Marks, like Karl, Groucho or "and Spencer". They just gave her that Russianised version of her name to make her more exotic!'

'Ever true, Orson,' laughed Arnold, and I was duly put in my place. When sitting at a king's table it is best not to initiate conversation or to make remarks which indicate opinions beyond those of the monarch in residence.

★

Many moons later in my life, I came across a real king in Africa. I was staying in a relatively ordinary hotel with my wife when we began to notice a distinguished-looking African breakfasting on his own in the self-service restaurant. At an adjacent table were four companions who had their eyes fixed on him. As soon as he had finished his cereal, one of them leapt up, approached his table and knelt in subservience before him, before taking his empty bowl away. His next course was served in the same way, with the obeisance made before the delivery of the food. All this was fine, except that it was taking place in a busy canteen with businessmen and staff all carrying on their ordinary ways. Nobody seemed to notice, except me. I was riveted by the notion of an African king and his courtiers carrying on as if they were in his *boma*, far out in the bush.

The routing went on quite a while and my wife kept on chiding me to eat my food rather than gaze at these seemingly archaic acts of courtly ritual. Eventually, much to my wife's embarrassment, I could not resist the temptation. When the courtiers were not watching the king, I went up to him and, bowing profusely but not going on bended knee, I introduced myself. His aged aristocratic face broke into a charming smile and he graciously indicated to me to take a chair next to him. I explained to him that I was an Englishman in Africa and I was fascinated by his presence in this rather pedestrian place. He explained he was here in the city for medical treatment and that his kingdom was in Zambia. He told me he had visited Bournemouth in England when he was a young man and had many happy memories there. I was moved and humbled by his dignity.

The idea of a king in exile had often crossed my mind during my time with Mr Welles. No wonder the prospect of playing King Lear always intrigued him as he grew older.

'You know, it was Thornton Wilder who first gave me great introductions into the Broadway theatre. Yes, I had already played Tybalt for Guthrie McClintic but Wilder came up one summer to the festival I'd arranged with Roger Hill at Woodstock, and he became a fan. Without him, I fear I might never have broken into that rather closed circle.'

We began to talk about Wilder's iconic story, The Bridge over the San Luis Rey, *which I loved but which was about chance and fate and destiny: things that had made huge impacts on the life of Mr Welles, as they do for all of us.*

Change is what few of us expect but which all of us experience.

23

Falstaff

They looked like Sir John Falstaff and Justice Shallow in the first scene of *Chimes at Midnight*. Mr Welles was obviously Falstaff, with cigar in hand and walking in an ungainly manner as though wearing heavy armour or uncomfortable chainmail; next to him sauntered the elegant Principe Alessandro Tasca Filangeri di Cutò, Count of Almerita, dressed immaculately in a well-cut suit and wearing beautiful handmade Italian shoes – what else would an Italian aristocrat wear?

His first cousin was the legendary Giuseppe di Lampedusa, author of *The Leopard*. His many relations were polemicists, poets, painters and photographers. He came from a family of artists. He had produced *Chimes at Midnight*.

★

'There live not three good men unhanged in England. And one of them is fat and grows old.'

Henry IV Pt 1 Act 2, Scene 4

★

I went to some pretentious forum on film production while I was in LA. These ignorant sons of bitches were informing me that Orson was 'difficult' to work with. What the hell did they know? None of them had even met him, but there they were.

Tasca's father was the stuff of legend. As a young man he had spent a brilliant but frivolous life, the centre of the golden world of the Sicilian aristocracy, travelling the length and breadth of Europe. But it was a time of social change with the First World War and the Russian Revolution turning Europe upside down. He espoused the socialist cause and without much difficulty squandered the family fortunes. Addicted to women and gambling, he married a Polish noblewoman, affectionately called Ama, by whom he had Alessandro Junior. Unbeknownst to the family he also sold off the Palazzo of Santa Margherita Belice, described in the novel *Il Gattopardo*, by Tomaso di Lampedusa.

The Red Prince, as he was remembered, died in poverty in Palermo in 1943, leaving Alessandro to make a living for himself, but the son always spoke with great affection and admiration for his father.

The two companions – Mr Welles, the American aristocrat (what the hell else was he?), and the Sicilian aristocrat – meandered into the edit suite led by me. Mr Welles took the main edit seat and I sat next to him, while Alessandro Tasca lurked on a sofa behind us.

'What is this material, Orson?' he enquired.

'Some footage we just shot in Yugoslavia for *The Deep*.'

'Good title,' said Tasca.

'Like yours!' jested Mr Welles, and roared with laughter.

I said nothing, but toyed with the notion that Alessandro's title meant 'Prince Pocket,' which kind of didn't have a ring of authority about it.

'Dorian, you are an Englishman, so I think you will find this story amusing. My ancestors were at the Bourbon Court in Palermo when King Ferdinand bestowed the Sicilian title of Duke of Bronte on Lord Nelson. Along with the title, he was given a palazzo and estates near Etna. Your mad King George III was very reluctant to acknowledge this title since it was foreign! Anyway, there was a man at that time, an impoverished vicar named Brunty. He was a big fan of the heroic Nelson, so he changed his name to Brontë. He had three daughters, Charlotte, Emily and Anne.'

'And I played Rochester to Joan Fontaine's Jane Eyre,' growled Mr Welles.

'The Battle of Shrewsbury scene in *Chimes at Midnight* is stunning,' I offered. They didn't react for a beat as the film continued to whir through the Moviola.

Then Mr Welles' hand flicked the edit handle into the halt position and the film stopped moving.

Silence. Heavy breathing.

'I'm glad you approve,' Mr Welles said.

'Of course. You captured the chaos of hand-to-hand fighting, its energy sapping efforts, its clumsiness, its ineptitude. Amazing. And the scene where that knight surrenders to the prone Falstaff. Wonderful. I really loved that film.'

'Why, thank you.'

'I've often wondered how combat was in the old days,' I continued. 'The sheer physical effort and exhaustion, staggering about in cumbersome armour carrying heavy swords or axes. Who was coming up behind you? The mind boggles.'

'I think men were physically in better shape in those days. You walked or rode everywhere. You hunted for your food and I think the knightly class trained in their military pursuits.'

'But still.'

Mr Welles relit his cigar.

'And the futility of it all. Killing for no purpose other than to win or survive the day.

'Exactly,' he said. 'Only a fool can think war is a good thing. Roosevelt didn't want war. Neither, as a matter of fact, did Churchill. And he had seen war. He had been in battle: not much more sophisticated than Shakespeare's time except there were rifles. They still rode on horses and carried swords and the opposition had spears. There is no glory in war.'

'Except we seem to honour those who survive it. They become heroes.'

He flicked the editing handle into forward and we continued to look at the mute footage shot back in Yugoslavia.

'Falstaff was Shakespeare's greatest character.'

'And you wonderfully simplified the story in *Chimes*. It set up the back history of Bolingbroke taking the crown from Richard II and his determination to secure his son's kingdom.'

'In a way, yes, but the story was really about the betrayal of friendship. Hal's rejection of Falstaff is one of the most moving scenes I have ever encountered. Everything in my movie leads to that. That awful moment when good old Falstaff is finally rejected.'

Then Mr Welles adjusted himself in his chair and, giving his voice a lighter timbre, delivered these immortal lines in the darkened room:

> I know thee not, old man: fall to thy prayers:
> How ill white hairs become a fool and jester!
> I have long dream'd of such a kind of man,
> So surfeit-swell'd, so loud and so profane:
> But, being awaked, I do despise my dream.

I was frozen, electrified, as this remarkable man spoke the remarkable words crafted 400 years before. The sneer in his voice was exactly right, indicating the unpleasantness of Prince Hal. That undisguised betrayal motivated by ambition.

I felt as though it should be me delivering to his Falstaff. I did, some months later, and betrayed him. Mr Welles demanded full loyalty and anything less than that was not acceptable.

I sat there in my editing chair next to his, looking at Falstaff himself. No disguises, no costumes, this was him incarnated. I was looking directly at 'this huge hill of flesh,' but the man I beheld was no sanguine coward. And I had a great love for him.

Welles was born to play Falstaff, not only because of the physical similarity but because of the rich voice, sonorous and amused, and the shared life experience. Both men lived long and too well, were at odds with the powers that were, and were constantly in debt. Both knew disappointment, and one of the most sublime moments in Welles' career is simply the expression on his face at the coronation of Henry V, when he cries out, 'God save thee, my sweet boy!' and the new king replies in those immortal words.

Falstaff is probably Shakespeare's greatest character, a real human being, 'warts and all.' He so dominates the *Henry IV* plays that, although Shakespeare promised he would return in *Henry V*, he reconsidered. The hugely fat knight would have sounded the wrong note in that heroic tale. We hear of his death from Mistress Quickly, as he 'babbl'd of green fields.' Like a smart, smarmy Hollywood executive, Prince Hal courted his own ambition and betrayed his true friend.

Mr Welles *was* Falstaff. As a young man he had conquered all that came before him. At the Battle of Shrewsbury, a knight meekly surrenders to Falstaff, awed by his leftover reputation, exactly as modern directors and cineastes wanted to get close to Welles, as if some of his magic would rub off on them.

Welles grew fat and in debt, took jobs unworthy of him, was trailed by sycophants and leeches, yet was loved and honoured by those who could see him clearly. And he battled on, Don Quixote, as well as Falstaff, always planning great things in his rolling imagination. It is significant that two of Mr Welles' greatest projects were Falstaff and Don Quixote. He had a great respect for Falstaff.

This reverence for the character increased over the years, and by the time Welles made *Chimes at Midnight*, his focus was entirely on the relationships between Falstaff, Hal and Henry IV. He believed that the core of the story was 'the betrayal of friendship.' Welles called Hal's rejection of Falstaff 'one of the greatest scenes ever written, so the movie is really a preparation for it. Everything prepares for it.' Throughout the film, Hal constantly turns his back on Falstaff, foreshadowing the film's ending.

That evening at dinner in an outside restaurant in Trastevere, we continued to talk about Falstaff. Mr Welles was typically assertive: 'The film was never intended as a lament for Falstaff, more for the death of Merry England, that conception, that myth which has been very real to the English-speaking world, and other countries of the Medieval epoch: the age of chivalry, of simplicity, of Maytime and all that. It is more than Falstaff who is dying. It's the old England dying and betrayed.'

'But many cultures are nostalgic for an idealised past,' said Alessandro.

'Not that it ever was ideal,' I interrupted. 'Peasants in the countryside spent most of their miserable lives slaving away to make some sort of living to prevent their children starving.'

'So speaks the young idealist. But the magical past is the central theme in Western culture. Even if "the good old days" never existed, the fact that we can conceive of such a world is, in fact, an affirmation of the human spirit. Maybe we can bring it all back. I think Falstaff is the greatest conception of a good man, the most completely good man, in all of drama. Thank you, William Shakespeare. The closer you get to Falstaff the less funny he seems. I've played him in the theatre where he is witty, more than a straight comic, and on film where he only becomes a clown deliberately. He's an innocent in some ways. He has faults for sure. He makes a joke out of his own cowardice against himself. He expects little and gets little.'

'He is like you, Orson. A man rejected.'

Mr Welles smiled wistfully at Alessandro and swigged down the rest of his Barolo. 'People always say that. So, I am also like Othello and Macbeth, or anyone else I've ever played? Poppycock, but it fits nicely in some goddam film student's presentation paper. Besides, I first played the part when I was at the Todd School in Illinois, then again when I was your age on Broadway when Houseman and I condensed the *History Plays* into a piece we called *Five Kings*. It was certainly the forerunner of *Chimes*, which, in fact, I first presented with Hilton Edwards and dear Micheál in Ireland.'

'And what a beautiful film you made, Orson. It is my favourite of all your work.'

'That's because I paid you money to produce it for me!'

'No,' said Alessandro, looking a little sad, 'you put into it many profound thoughts from you, not Shakespeare, about old age and mortality, betrayal, friendship, the meaning of honour, father-hood and what it means to be a king.'

Silence fell at our table while the noise of happy diners on this warm Roman night continued around us like flocks of chattering starlings. Mr Welles wiped his brow with his napkin, dug into his cigar box and pulled out another Montecristo. He took off the paper band and stuck it in his mouth. Then he lit a match. 'It was a personal film and I put a lot of myself into it.'

The match was burning out, so he tried to light the cigar but failed and threw the dying match away. Then he lit another, which burnt vigorously, and he forcefully sucked on his cigar as the embers glowed in the darkness.

'In *Chimes*, you let the characters' faces say everything, not the radical camera angles that are your normal signature.'

'True.'

'You did the same in *Ambersons*,' enthused Alessandro.

He was right. Those two films were different from Welles' normal Gothic style. The first time I had seen *Chimes* was at the Everyman in Hampstead, that haven of foreign films in the 1960s. The film captivated me as much as *Kane* had captivated me, in all its complexity, some years before.

Alessandro bade us goodnight and disappeared into those laby-rinthine back streets of Trastevere where the real Roman 'mob' had existed since Renaissance times. Mr Welles and I ambled along to our car, his giant shadow reflecting along the freshly washed cobble stones. I stepped ahead of him to open the car and, looking back, enjoyed his great silhouette as he drew on his cigar and exhaled the smoke into the heavy night air. The smoke curled lazily around his head and up into the darkness.

We must have looked like that spellbinding scene in Carol Reed's *Odd Man Out*, where the mortally wounded James Mason stumbles through the back streets of Belfast led by the nimble and tiny Irishman, F.J. McCormick.

He slumped into our trusty Mini and I drove him home. 'That was an evening of profundities,' he laughed, 'I find Alessandro more than depressing when he drinks red wine. Maybe it's a longing for the past, or a longing for the glory days in Sicily. God knows. Falstaff was fun and full of mischief. Moping about his demise is not the only thing. The trouble is people who feel sorry for me keep on likening me to him. I am an actor, for God's sake, an entertainer trying to entertain people.'

We passed the dark and brooding Castel San Angelo as we crossed the Tiber into central Rome. 'We shot a lot of *Cagliostro* up there. My, that was a fun time. I was paid a lot of money and dear old Gregory Ratoff was a sweetheart. Didn't have a clue.'

'Wasn't he the director?'

'Director? My God, he couldn't direct the bloody traffic, let alone a movie. But he was a sweet man and the shoot was one long party. I don't think I've ever enjoyed myself so much in my life. The war was ended, Roma was *La Citta Aperta* in so many ways. And we were the first American-financed movie in town. It was a ball.'

After Mr Welles rolled out of the car and disappeared into the hotel, I drove slowly home down the slope from the Via Veneto back to the Piazza di Spagna. I passed the illuminated Trevi Fountain, where a group of tourists were sitting. Their underlit faces could have been from any century of Rome's many, and I imagined Mr Welles as a Renaissance cardinal being carried in a sedan chair past them back to his palazzo, his servants struggling with his immense weight. I thought that his body was beyond ridiculous, it was now sublime, like a rare and monstrous wild beast, lonely and melancholy even. Like Falstaff, he feared nothing, not even his inevitable death, 'Thou'lt forget me, when I am gone.'

How wrong can you be? Those of us who were lucky enough to spend time with him will surely remember him with all his wit and wisdom and wiles.

24

LUNAR LANDING

Neil Armstrong stepped out onto the surface of the moon at the Sea of Tranquillity on 21 July 1969. I will never forget it. President Jack Kennedy's promise made at his inauguration eight long and traumatic years before had come to pass. The crappy old television set in the small lobby of the Hotel Piazza di Spagna crackled, and the unclear black and white image revealed itself as Armstrong gingerly placed his left foot onto the white ground. Our hearts were beating as we watched, mesmerised. What was going to happen? Was he safe? Was the ground on which he placed his feet solid?

'One small step for man, one giant leap for mankind,' announced the astronaut calmly.

And I thought about mankind as I stood there in a small group of people, some of whom had walked in from the street. There I was, in the middle of the suffocating streets of Rome in high summer, where Caesars had strolled, barbarians had conquered and Popes had ruled, in the midst of the Roman mob who had existed almost from the beginning of our civilisation, and witnessing with them this new step into the unknown. I was glad to be in Rome, of all places, and glad that the ancient city could be part of the earth's future. We were mankind, all rooting for that one man far away from us on a desolate planet.

'*Un passo giante per umanita*!' shouted Andrea, the hotel manager, and we all shouted 'Bravo! Bravo!' and clapped like the Roman crowds when a gladiator performed an extraordinary feat.

The next morning, as we sat over the Prevost editing once more, I asked Mr Welles if he had watched the events of the previous evening.

'Sure. But we should be careful with how we proceed into space. I take the moon very seriously and its influence upon us. Women are controlled by her, their cycles, their moods, their very beings are all dictated by her. No wonder she was the female god. Beware of the waxing moon. She is so fragile; your gaze must be pure otherwise you will be fated with misfortune.' With those mysterious words, he grabbed the control handle on the machine, spun the material back to where we had started and asked me to make a cut on the frame he had stopped.

We never talked about the moon or the space programme again, although his words 'fated with misfortune' somewhat troubled me. Did they apply to him or me?

★

Man's arrival on the moon was the product of Kennedy's drive and his famous 'We choose to go to the Moon' speech. 'We set sail on this new sea because there is new knowledge to be gained, and new rights to be won, and they must be won and used for the progress of all people.'

Those inspiring words made us all believe, but sadly the Kennedys finally faced a Faustian payback of their own, which was brutal and final, and it was only in later years that we believers in Camelot learnt that our heroes were somewhat tarnished. The glamorous knights and their ladies, in whom we had all believed in were full of human frailties and no better than all of us.

★

Sidney Poitier was lunching at a nearby table in a restaurant just off the Via Veneto. He came over and greeted Mr Welles. He was probably the biggest star in the world then. Already an Oscar winner for *Lilies of the Field*, he had just completed three hugely successful movies: *Guess Who's Coming to Dinner*, *To Sir, with Love* and *In the Heat of the Night*, opposite Rod Steiger. Mr Welles shook his hand and said how much he loved *A Patch of Blue*.

The strikingly handsome Bahamian smiled graciously and thanked him. They then discussed *Othello*, which Poitier much admired, telling us that he had turned down the part for NBC. 'They wanted a Sidney Poitier persona to play Othello. I didn't think it was right for me.'

'You're right, you're too nice for Othello. At least that's your image. Or you could have played the Moor against your character. You couldn't do worse than Larry Olivier, who was awful.'

'Like a West Indian London bus driver,' I concurred.

'He just made Othello into a laughing stock,' laughed Mr Welles.

I met Poitier years later at a showing of *A Patch of Blue* at a British Academy Award ceremony for the English director, Guy Green. 'You were lucky to spend quality time with a legend,' he told me. 'We are all in his debt for his work with the Harlem theatre. It gave us all hope.'

Mr Welles always said that one of the main strands of racism was a class thing. The fact was that the majority of African Americans had been rural agricultural workers and, even when they came north to work in the great industrial cities, they were considered working class and therefore looked down on. He talked of his so-called 'Voodoo' production of *Macbeth*, which he opened at the Lafayette Theatre in Harlem on 14 April 1936, when he was just 20. Three weeks later, he came of age and could vote:

'*Macbeth* is all about foreboding and fate and witches, so I thought, that's it, West Indian voodoo, or *muti*, as it's called in Africa, had come over on the slave ships and was a natural for an all-African play. It worked. My old buddy John Houseman had been made head of the Negro Theatre Unit and called me. He offered me $23.86 a week salary, that's what I pay you! Of course, money wasn't the point, the point was to release people from their petit bourgeois notions about black people. We set the play in Haiti in the time of Henri Cristophe, the former slave who declared himself king in the time of the Napoleonic wars.'

Money wasn't the point, I concurred. Mr Welles never paid me properly. I was given cash in various currencies to survive on and that was it. It didn't bother me at all. After all, I was the sorcerer's apprentice and life was good.

I cast the formidable Jack Carter as the Scottish king. He'd played the original Porgy. He was a man apart. He was big, strong and menacing. I was scared of him, really. He wasn't just an actor, he was well connected in Harlem and I suspect was up to all sorts of skulduggery – perfect for Macbeth!

'At the time I was doing theatre work on Broadway in the '30s, I was just a kid. I would wait till after a show when I was in full costume and then I would make my criticisms. The older actors took it better from whatever mature character I was playing than from a 20-year-old boy!'

25

BLACK MAGIC AND THE BLACK DAHLIA

'We had more fun making that picture than any I can remember. Gregory was a hopeless director but a lot of fun. He'd let me direct my own pieces but screwed it all up in the edit. You know he acted a bit and played the confused producer in *All About Eve*.'

We were stuck in traffic outside the Palazzo Quirinale, which is what had triggered his musings. 'That palazzo is enormous. One of the biggest in the world built by Renaissance Popes, lived in by the Kings of Risorgimento in Italy and now the President of the Italian Republic. God knows how Michele Scalera, the Italian producer, and Ed Small managed to negotiate that we could use it as a double for Versailles! Actually, that's a lie. I do know. Michele was an incredibly powerful man in Italy, or perhaps I should call him "*Commendatore*" – everybody did. A good producer needs muscle and he had it in spades. He had been even more influential in Mussolini's day. So we shot in the Scalera Studios in Rome and Venice, since Cinecittà was a refugee camp.

'He even organised an audience with the Pope for me. I swept away from here in a black limousine to the Vatican. As we drove in, the Swiss Guard just waved us through. We walked through room after room adorned with huge religious paintings, Raphael's probably. When I was ushered into the Pope's study, Michele knelt and kissed his hand. He then introduced me and I bowed and also kissed his papal ring. Meeting the leader of the Roman Catholic Church, the direct descendant of St Peter, is humbling.

'Pacelli was a Roman aristocrat, through and through, highly educated, sophisticated. He'd been Pope all through the war and had to deal with the Nazis as well as Mussolini. I wanted to ask him about those chaotic years in Italy when the Germans invaded after the fall of Mussolini. And all he asked me was if I knew whether Irene Dunne was going to get a divorce! I ask you, there I am with one of the most important Popes in modern history, a man who played an important role during the Second World War, asking me about an actress in LA that I had never met, as though LA was a little village in Italy and I was the local priest.'

'She was a keen Catholic, by all accounts,' I suggested.

'Yes, maybe that was it. And that was the end of it. Just Irene Dunne, no discussion about the Nazis, or the treatment of Jews in Italy, or anything else.

'After the war, the Quirinale had been left vacant and we had just finished shooting the last scenes when the ceremonial guard arrived to escort the new President of the Italian Republic into his official residence. We used the Pope's bedroom to double for Marie Antoinette's bedroom, the hall of mirrors for the hall of mirrors.

'I was playing Cagliostro. It was fun. We only finished filming the day the newly-elected President of the Italian Republic moved into his official residence.'

★

At Fono Roma, as we walked in, an Italian journalist rushed up to us, microphone in hand, with a photographer in tow. 'I do research on why you left the USA in 1949. Some people say you left the States because of the Black Dahlia scandal. What you say? Any comment?'

I didn't even know what the guy was talking about, but clearly it affected Mr Welles. He went white in the face, froze, and faced up to the journalist in a confrontational way. 'What the hell are you talking about? Check your facts, you sonofabitch!'

He was angry. Sweating. He turned and strode on, 'Come on, Dorian, we have work to do. I've been accused of a lot of things but I draw the line at murder.'

I was in shock at his anger. We hurried into the cutting room and both sat down. He was breathing heavily. I said nothing.

'What kind of shit is that? How low can they sink?'

'What's it about?' I naively asked.

'Run the footage,' Mr Welles demanded, which I duly did.

In the darkness, he talked, 'It was some gruesome murder in LA while I was still living there. Some poor kid – Elizabeth Short, I think was her name – some kind of hooker, come actress, come whatever, was found murdered. Her body was cut totally in half, drained of blood. It was a sensational case. Macabre. Anybody who was anybody was considered a suspect by the gutter press in LA. They thought anyone who was a movie star or moved in those circles was perverted or mixed up in some way. Even Louis B. Mayer was a suspect. They said I was a magician obsessed with sawing people in half! And I applied for my passport in January 1947 when the hysteria was at its height.'

No sawn-in-half bodies were found when I was in Rome, nor in Vienna, nor in London, nor in Venice, so I can safely assume that Mr Welles had nothing to do with it.

26

ASSISI

'Is that Saint Francis?'

'Yes, Your Holiness,' I calmly replied.

'Happy Birthday, Saint Francis.'

'Thank you, Your Holiness, how did you know?'

'I am omnipotent and omniscient, dear boy.'

It was the Wizard from Wisconsin on the line, like the Pope from Rome to his friar general in Assisi. Mr Welles would have made a formidable medieval pope, his voice booming through St Peter's. He'd been a good Cardinal Wolsey in Fred Zinnemann's *A Man for all Seasons*. His sarcastic, 'Pray, by all means' to Paul Schofield as Thomas More was perfect innuendo.

'Is Saint Francis having a nice time looking after all the little birds?' roared the giant voice down the telephone.

I had taken the weekend off and driven up from Rome into Umbria and the dramatically located town of Assisi, looking out from its viewpoint across the Perugian Plain. I had feasted my eyes on the Giotto frescoes, glimmering dimly on the cavernous ceiling of the exquisite cathedral, and walked in the adjoining colonnades and courtyards and, for a few precious hours, set aside the constant tensions of working with Mr Welles. He was always a man in a hurry, a man of urges, a man with dreams that needed to be born, nurtured and matured, like fruit from a tree.

The telephone had rung harshly in my ear, waking me abruptly. It happened to be the morning of my birthday. 'Good morning, Saint Francis! Happy birthday! I'll expect you on Monday.'

'Of course, Holy Father,' I replied, continuing the joke. As the phone went down I heard him saying to Oja, 'What the hell is the boy doing rubbernecking in Assisi?' followed by the shrill laugh of Oja.

'Get him back, he works for you!'

So, the remark about the birds was at first charming, then caustic. His preoccupations naturally were the only things that mattered to him. Often people who had worked with him were scattered by the road like chaff in the wind. I would probably be one of them.

After breakfast, I climbed up to the great castle that overlooked Assisi, the Maggiore. Driving back, I paused to read the names in an Allied graveyard and to look at the cathedral in Arezzo, so badly damaged by that grim fighting in 1944 across the breadth of Italy, which has been much forgotten. A strange historical cocktail stretches across both Umbria and Tuscany: late medieval ecclesiastical buildings, churches, cathedrals, monasteries, high Renaissance country villas and stately homes, and suddenly brutish reminders of 1944 disguised as tranquil manicured graveyards of young men, fighting and dying as men like Mr Welles indulged themselves in California.

To say your grandfather fell at Omaha Beach or Saipan or Guadalcanal somehow sounds more apt than Tuscany or Umbria, those fertile gardens of the Italian Renaissance where only artists, writers and lovers should walk. Even the name of the victorious general of the time, Mark Clark, with due respect to his memory, sounds like a chain of fast-food outlets. Hardly Hannibal or Belisarius, whose ghostly Carthaginian and Byzantine armies still stalked these hills.

Returning, I detoured round Rome to the coast and Anzio, that precarious beachhead created to ensure the swift encirclement of the city. Walking among those immaculately manicured graves and gazing out to sea, I imagined the Allied fleets firing rapidly, salvo after salvo, at the entrenched German positions. Positions that threatened the tenuous foothold the Allied infantry held this close to Rome. The German defences had been so thin at one point that one British unit in a jeep drove straight through their lines and were driving straight up the main road to the Eternal City when they suddenly realised nobody was with them and had to run back.

★

'You know Cecil B. De Mille apparently reshot the beginning of the film he was making after he'd screened Kane? He wanted to copy my style. I was flattered!'

'Do you know the "Ready when you are, Mr De Mille" story?' I asked.

'No. Tell me.'

'So, they are shooting The Ten Commandments. *An epic. Cast of thousands. Three cameras. Huge scene, armies advance into battle. At the end, De Mille calls "cut" and checks with his camera crews.*

'"Camera 1, How was it?"

'"Just checking, Mr De Mille. A hair in the gate unfortunately."

'"Camera 2?"

'"We had a focus problem, Mr De Mille."

'"OK, Camera 3?"

'Camera 3 was far away in the distance and De Mille had to call them through a loud hailer. No answer. He called again. In the far distance a faint voice replied, "Ready when you are Mr De Mille." They had not even turned over!'

There was a silence for a moment, then he burst into laughter, repeating my line, 'Ready when you are Mr De Mille.'

After that, whenever we finished turning over a shot I used to call out, 'Ready when you are Mr De Welles!' Sometimes he laughed, sometimes he smiled and sometimes he glowered, depending on his mood. The Italian crews were oblivious to the joke.

He was a moody king and could be venomous if crossed. Messengers were often executed.

★

At the end of August, we shot some film on that wonderful Italian phenomenon, their uniquely expressive and illustrative way of using their hands as they speak. We hired an unmarked van, blacked out the windows like some police surveillance team, and parked in any number of locations around Rome. By using telephoto, or long lenses, we focused in on those wonderfully expressive hands as they danced, drooped, came alive, nodded agreement, implored, supplicated, approved, or just plain died.

Watching the silent footage in the dark viewing room was hilarious and there was another film to be made of our eager faces, lit by our own material, watching what those silent strangers' hands meant. We understood every word.

I suspect that if you tied an Italian's hands together he would fall silent.

Two hands in prayer moving up and down mean 'I ask you?' or 'What can you say?' or 'What an idiot!' One hand dangling with the thumb and index finger connected means, 'Tell me another,' or 'Do me a favour.' Two hands held separately open with palms upwards means, 'What did he think he was doing?' or 'What do you think?' or 'I give up.' One hand held up from the elbow in supplication means 'What can I say?' or 'I ask you, were they crazy?' One hand dangling and rotating with fingers together means 'F*** you, you arsehole!' or 'What a waste of time.' Two hands held up in a sign of surrender means 'What more can I say?' or 'What a disaster. They are bloody idiots!' And so on and so on.

The worst one is a hand held on top of your head, with your index finger and little finger pointed upwards. This denotes horns or '*cornuto*' (cuckold): your wife is being unfaithful. This is a serious matter for an Italian – men can be as unfaithful as they want, but women must be faithful. This is the ultimate insult for the vain Italian man. I once made the sign to some singularly bad driver who had cut me up and was pursued for miles, fearing I was going to be beaten up, till I lost him in traffic going round the Colosseum.

★

'I've always been more interested in experiment than accomplishment.'

27

King Louis XVIII at the Palace of Caserta

In September, Mr Welles was cast as Louis XVIII, the inept Bourbon king put back onto the throne of France by the Allies, England, Russia, Austria–Hungary and Prussia, after Napoleon Bonaparte had abdicated in 1814 and been exiled to the island of Elba. The production was called *Waterloo* and starred Rod Steiger as Napoleon and Christopher Plummer as the Duke of Wellington. It was an American-Italian-Russian co-production, with the great battle re-enacted on the rolling plains of Ukraine rather than on its original site, just outside Brussels.

Mr Welles was chauffeured down to Naples, where his scenes were to be shot, and I was instructed to follow in my little car. The Palace of Versailles was to be reproduced by the great Neapolitan Bourbon Palace of Caserta, Allied headquarters of General Mark Clark during the Italian campaign in 1943. It is a vast, grey stone building which, in its sheer scale, is one of the few palaces in Europe that in any way matches the vanity of Versailles.

There was a marvellous scene where the Marshals of France, led by Marshal Ney, played by Dan O'Herlihy, take their leave of the fleeing king and he leaves the deserted palace in a carriage to escape the oncoming Napoleon. We rehearsed his departure scene, where he walks alone down the great staircase of the palazzo.

'Come down the stairs with me, Dorian. Help me if I fall.'

So, slowly we descended, step by step. He was steadying himself with a cane. Sure enough, he missed his footing and stumbled forward. The crew members who were watching gasped. I threw myself forward and managed to get under his great torso as he lost his balance. Effectively he was splayed across my back.

I am strong, but the downward pressure on me was enormous, something like 300lb. We must have looked like some gigantic tortoise. I managed to slide him back onto his buckled feet and pushed him upright. There he stood, sweating profusely, caked in his character's make-up with a false nose and powdered wig, very much the King of France.

Mr Welles was magnificent in the role, small though it was, and the silence as he came down that great marble staircase, the only sound his stick as it struck each marble step, was electrifying. It was as if a king really was departing his palace.

The film was directed by the Stalin protégé Sergei Bondarchuk, who was working with largely American actors and an Italo-Russian film crew. He spoke not a word of English, so communication was somewhat chaotic. Bondarchuk had learnt his trade in the cavernous Mosfilm Studios, built on the orders of the film buff Joseph Stalin. Their scale is gigantic, cavernous stages lurking in freezing gloom, Kafkaesque corridors running for miles past 1,000 faceless unmarked doors, overly painted actresses hurrying to meet hard-faced unsmiling film crews.

★

It was along one of these endless corridors, many years after I had known Mr Welles, that I became aware that all was not well within me as I struggled with the pace and the freezing temperatures. It was snowing as I stumbled cautiously back to my hotel. I called for a doctor and waited nervously, dreading, this snowy Friday night in an anonymous room in an anonymous hotel, what Russian medical practice was like.

After an interminable time, a young female Russian doctor who spoke no English arrived, accompanied by a very good stand-in for Ian Fleming's ghastly Rosa Klebb. She could have been the doctor's grandmother, with her hooded eyes and massive forearms. She also spoke no English and proceeded to pull out of her medical bag a hypodermic syringe that looked as if it had last been used at Stalingrad.

After some instructions from the doctor, who then left, she turned me over like a piece of meat and stabbed me violently with the needle. I felt the drug entering my body painfully. Then two ambulance men came in and stretchered me downstairs through the hotel lobby into a waiting ambulance. I waved weakly at the concierge as I departed. God knows what he thought was going on. I lay alone in the blue-lit back of the ambulance. Then I heard people getting into the front, the engine started and we moved off.

I had no idea where I was going – nor did anybody else on the planet, not my family, my friends or my enemies. The journey seemed to take forever on the soft, silent snow-covered streets of Moscow. I began to feel drowsy as the effects of the giant injection set in. I fell into a deep sleep.

After what seemed an hour, the sliding window connecting me to the driver's cabin was suddenly smashed back and the nurse was shouting my name, '*Gospodin* Bond, are you alive?'

I sat bolt upright on the stretcher, restrained though I was by blankets and straps. They laughed as I settled back down, repeating the 'Mr Bond' name, enjoying the James Bond thing since he was known as Russia's greatest enemy. I realised they thought I had died while they smoked in the front.

After an hour, we arrived at an enormous snow-covered flood-lit sanatorium and I was taken into a brightly lit examination room where I was given a number of blood tests and a further injection. The doctor who came in to examine me was wearing overalls which were severely blood-spattered. Clearly, he had just been operating on some poor sod without much success. But he spoke good English and seemed to know what he was doing.

I later discovered this was the best hospital in Moscow, where they had performed open heart surgery on Boris Yeltsin and treated all the Soviet elite.

Now more versions of Rosa Klebb took over and I was taken up some floors in a lift that swayed on its wires, and wheeled into a corridor, bigger and wider and longer than those at Mosfilm Studios. It was night by now, and all was silent as I was put into a ward. The nurses, in their Great Patriotic War uniforms, left me to my silence. I lay there thinking that although this was Moscow, this must be the best facility, probably for senior party officials and rocket scientists.

A voice spoke to me out of the darkness in fluent English, asking me how I was and what I was doing there. He explained he also had heart trouble and he was a rocket scientist. I smiled in the darkness.

The following day, I was moved into a single room with en suite bathroom. It could have been Brezhnev's hospital room, since it had its own balcony looking onto a snow-covered pine forest, Persian carpets on the floor, oil paintings with ornate gilt frames on the walls, a bath which looked like something out of the battleship *Potemkin* and a direct dialling telephone to anywhere in the world.

Unfortunately, I was constantly visited by the Rosa Klebb-type nurses who continually took blood tests from the tips of my fingers. I began to dread the sound of their trolleys loaded with syringes as they patrolled the corridors.

My tests continued and I was given a heart monitor to wear constantly. I was allowed to walk in the snow-covered grounds. I felt like a prisoner as I watched the guards at the gates in the far distance and looked back up at the menacing building in which I was housed. The library filled much of my time. It was magnificent, with volumes in a myriad of languages. I resorted to Galsworthy to pass the hours. I later discovered that his writing was considered a perfect picture of bourgeois life.

After some days, I was released and returned in haste to my family.

★

Sitting in Mr Welles' trailer, with him fully dressed up as one of the last of the Bourbons, powdered wig and all, perspiring heavily in all his regalia, I thought how ill-suited was a man as strong as he to play a weak and vacillating king. But he did it well, measuring perfectly that fine balance between prevarication and arrogance that weak leaders display.

I thought often of Mr Welles on that staircase in Naples during my days in Moscow. The staircases and grand halls of the Kremlin were on a gigantic scale, designed to intimidate rather than to impress. There was no logical connection; maybe it was merely the scale of the buildings, or the fact that it was Italians who built the Kremlin in the fifteenth century along the lines of one of their fortresses.

★

We talked of Naples and he told me he had been there during the war as a correspondent and, coming ashore, had paid a Neapolitan youth to carry his suitcase. On arriving at his hotel, he had turned round to the boy and had been shocked to see that he had no suitcase. The boy summoned another boy to ask him the whereabouts of the missing case and the second boy, quite casually, pointed to a third boy, smaller than them both, struggling along with the enormous suitcase.

'Ecco,' said the senior boy with a smile and took the money to share down the pecking order.

'That's the Italian way,' explained Mr Welles, 'Delegate to ensure you do no work yourself, but profit from it!'

I've since learnt that this was not a uniquely Italian trait.

★

In later years, I visited Hartwell House, the fairly modest (certainly by Bourbon standards) country house where Louis XVIII spent most of his days in exile during the Napoleonic era. I stood on its pleasant English democratic lawns and wondered how he and his simpering courtiers must have compared it to the larger-than-life vistas and wide terraces of Versailles.

Mr Welles was big enough for Versailles, but not Louis XVIII.

★

'Did you know that Louis XIV's wigs must have been constantly full of builders' dust, as work on the great palace went on during most of his seemingly endless reign. He reigned for about fifty years, so long that he was succeeded by his grandson who then reigned another fifty years. They really brought on the French Revolution under the unfortunate Louis XVI. The Sun King so centralised his power that he insisted on all the leading aristocrats of France coming to Versailles to live there next to him, so he could keep an eye on them. The only problem was the accommodation. They were put into little apartments next to each other, like a rabbit warren. It must have been awful. Cheek by jowl with everyone listening to what you said. No privacy. Meanwhile, France fell into poverty because nobody at Versailles knew what was going on outside Versailles. How could you? Rich and poor: the eternal conflict of mankind.'

★

What I have realised, in hindsight, is that Mr Welles was taking these relatively insignificant parts to pay for his lifestyle. I suppose he had to support his Italian wife, Paola Mori, and their daughter Beatrice in London, plus Oja and the small entourage, including Ann Rogers and me. His hotel bills alone must have been astronomical, but I guess they were, on the whole, picked up by each production as he went into it.

Each job he did as an actor seemed small and not large enough to ensure financial security for a long period of time. He was like an upmarket gypsy, living from hand to mouth.

★

'*Cornelia Lunt was in her mid-nineties when I first met her back in Chicago. She was a beautiful woman, in fact; clearly, she had grown into her looks and when she was young she might not have been so attractive. A big nose, for example, may not be so appealing when you are a youth but in middle age it may become a mark of distinction! She had been a leading member of society during the Civil War and knew many of the main characters in that national tragedy. She would quote Lincoln on a first-hand basis. Remarkable. She also went to London and met Benjamin Disraeli and Gladstone and all sorts of eminent Victorians.*'

*The next day in the edit suite I was singing '*Cornelia, you're breaking my heart*' to the Simon and Garfunkel track when Mr Welles walked in. He ignored me imperiously, grunting, '*Let's get back to work.*' My joke was not accepted.*

28

A Secret Place

'I'm going to show you a secret place,' said Mr Welles. 'We leave tomorrow. Oja will join us there.'

Asolo, a small town – walled village, really – was nestled in the pre-Alpine foothills just north of Treviso, overlooking, on a clear day, the Venetian Plain. So, with Mr Welles in my little car, we proceeded north along the Aurelian Way, across the Apennines, Lombardy and into Veneto, the inland region surrounding Venice. We stopped on the way only once for lunch in a country trattoria. The locals all stared at Mr Welles, knowing his face and knowing he was famous, but not knowing who he was. Mr Welles ordered a Cagnina di Romagna which we drank chilled. Then we ate polenta, cotechino and lenticchia, and it was more than filling.

'Cotechino is really a hot, cooked salami,' he explained, 'and, you know, polenta rather than pasta is the staple in this part of Italy.'

After two double expressos, we drove towards Asolo, as Mr Welles talked on. 'Asolo has been a secret for many years. It's a small paradise owned in the Renaissance by a queen of Cyprus, then in the past 100 years, Robert Browning, Eleonora Duse and Freya Stark settled there at different times.'

These 'secret' places are harder and harder to find. Everybody goes to them once some celebrity travel writer has freeloaded for a few days at the expense of a glossy magazine, and the place is ruined forever with baying voices, and the 'well-kept secret' is out. Once a magic place, wherever it may be in the world, appears in a Sunday paper travel section or in a glossy magazine, the secret is no longer a secret. The innocence and authenticity is ruined forever and the place is never the same again. As the population of the world multiplies and accelerates there will be no secret places, no unspoilt beaches, no small harbours where only local fishermen ply their trade. Asolo was like that then.

With a small piazza and colonnaded walkways along its narrow streets, it provided a cooler alternative to the heat of Venice in the summer and a country feel as it looked out across the small rolling hills of neat walled fields and orchards punctuated occasionally by sharply vertical cypress trees.

If you look at Italian Renaissance portraits, for example the *Mona Lisa*, you will see idyllic rural scenes in the background. I always thought these visuals came from the imagination of the painter. Far from it. In Asolo, and places like it in Tuscany, these idyllic scenes are real, as if some great artist had laid them out.

The Italian sense of aesthetics is deep within them, ingrained. From architecture, Roman, Renaissance or modern, to design, or just to how people look, it is all around you. Even truck drivers look cool in their immaculate T-shirts.

In Asolo there are a number of private villas looking out over the valley, one of which had the name Freya Stark on the doorbell. She was the well-known English traveller, writer and eccentric, last in the line stretching back to Lady Hester Stanhope, who had set up house in the Lebanon in Napoleonic times. The next-door villa was owned by the Earl of Iveagh, head of the Guinness family, who had set up house there with Eleanora Duse, Italy's answer to Sarah Bernhardt and former mistress of the patriot and proto-Fascist, Gabriele D'Annunzio, in the 1920s.

Beyond this was the Hotel Cipriani, another former private villa, owned by the Guinness family, now partners in the Cipriani Hotel Group. It was really like a private house with a superb restaurant and its own terraced garden. The view from each bedroom window could have been from the background of a Leonardo portrait, or even a scene from a Corot landscape.

I should explain why Mr Welles wanted to be in Asolo. We were to do more work on Carter de Haven's CBS special and he planned to film parts of *The Merchant of Venice*. Who better to adapt Shakespeare than Mr Welles, the adaptor of three of his works already? And the restaurant in the hotel was superlative.

Charles Gray was to play Antonio, Anthony Ainley would play Bassanio, Jonathan Lynn would play Tubal and a young actress, whose name I don't recall, would play Jessica. I was to play Launcelot Gobbo, and Mr Welles, of course, would play Shylock.

Charles Gray was an urbane actor, later to achieve notoriety in the Bond films as Blofeld, James Bond's deadly opponent. He was tall with an elegant voice and a malicious sense of humour. He travelled with his young West Indian manservant, who doubled as his lover.

Jonathan Lynn, who happened to be the nephew of the Israeli statesman Abba Eban, was brilliant, witty, enthusiastic, modest and fun. He later wrote the TV series *Yes Minister* and *Yes, Prime Minister*, and became a successful director in Hollywood, making the delightful *My Cousin Vinny*, among other films. Anthony Ainley, later well-known for his role as the Master in *Doctor Who*, was quiet and could never grasp the banter we indulged in with Charles Gray.

We were an unlikely group and only behaved when Mr Welles appeared like a dominating headmaster. Charles, the oldest but the most mischievous of us all, would pull faces behind Mr Welles, but could switch in a flash to acting mode, delivering wonderfully mannered passages of iambic pentameters.

I managed, with the help of the hotel manager, to secure the next-door Guinness villa as our interior location. The exteriors we would do in Venice itself. So, we started shooting in our mid-eighteenth-century costumes, waistcoats, frock coats, tricorn black hats and wigs. We shot scenes all around the narrow streets, discreet bridges and small piazzas hidden behind the main tourist venues of Venice.

One image haunts me to this day. The Piazza San Giorgio, in front of the great San Giorgio Church, faces out across the main lagoon to the Doge's Palace. It is laid out with enormous black and white flagstones, worn out over the centuries by the winds and the buckled shoes of merchants going about their business. There, Mr Welles shot an almost balletic scene with all the actors dressed in black cloaks, white Venetian masks and black tricorn hats, which captured the mystery, menace and power of that great trading city, lying in its lagoons at the head of the Adriatic Sea. I never saw this footage and wonder whether it was ever used.

Maybe I am owed residual fees by the Screen Actors' Guild.

Mr Welles should have made a version of *The Merchant of Venice* to end all versions, and he touched on it in this small abbreviated version we performed together.

His *Othello* captured completely the idea of the Venetian Empire and its Mediterranean outposts, his use of locations was flawless, and the image of caged Iago, played by Micheál Mac Liammóir, hangs in the memory. This *Merchant of Venice* suggested the sophistication and machinations of the capital of that merchant empire. Venice, above all other cities, was created by merchants. Merchants are often maligned in history, giving way to the more glamorous generals and statesmen. But it was they who fostered and supported art and architecture, right through the ages from the Italian merchant princes of the high Renaissance down to the American colossi of the late nineteenth century.

★

'The Kennedys liked the ladies. No doubt about that. Camelot was a romantic fantasy thought up by their writers. And it worked! My God, it worked! All of your generation who voted them in thought them pure as driven snow. Nothing of the sort!

'Marlene told me a story only last year. She had been in Washington and was informed that the president would like to meet her. She had replied that she had an awards ceremony in the evening. That would be fine, she was advised. Ushered into the White House, the president led her straight to the bedroom, undressed, had sex with her wasting no time, got dressed again and proceeded back

to the Oval Office. That says as much about Marlene and her self-confidence as it does about Jack Kennedy.

'Oh, and as he left, he asked her if she had had sex with his father, to which she replied no.'

Mr Welles was talking to me in the 1960s and I was taken aback. It was only some years later that his words turned out to be the truth.

★

I often think it unfortunate that Mr Welles never had an artistic benefactor. He made films intelligently and cheaply, with a small crew and little waste; the investments would have been relatively modest; the participation enormous fun and the potential rewards large. Nowadays he would have thrived in this world of indie films.

While we were shooting in Venice, Welles stayed at the other Hotel Cipriani on Giudecca Island, opposite the main city. It has a gigantic swimming pool which nobody can account for. The best explanation is that a pool of, say, 50ft by 30ft was originally asked for. The builder perhaps misunderstood this and made it 50 yards by 30 yards, which is totally out of proportion to the fairly small hotel garden and grounds. Another architectural anomaly like the National Hotel in Moscow, without the terror element.

It's small stories like Stalin and the architects of the Moscow hotel that tell us more about history than all the dates and facts we learn. The fact is that Churchill and Stalin ran most of the war while inebriated.

In the West, we are taught in our polite schools about ordered history: that the Middle Ages came to an end roughly in the middle of the fifteenth century, coinciding approximately with the Renaissance in Italy, the stabilisation of the monarchy in England and, latterly, the discovery of the Americas. Not so. The three events are not linked, just coincidental, and if you had lived at that time you would hardly have been aware of these significant sea changes. Chance and missed opportunities have as much a role to play in events as social movements. So when the West refused to shore up the moderate White Russians, the result was the eventual victory of Lenin. So Stalin, the Georgian gangster, his menacing henchmen and a legion of imitators following in his bloody footsteps have perpetuated the ground rules of Genghis Khan to this day. It is ironic, again in the West, that the practice of diplomacy and the study of history is, by and large, conducted by urbane, civilised, mild men who have no grasp of the moods, lusts, alcoholic urges, and corrupt cravings that drive on most national leaders outside of the most evolved democracies. And democracy? Hitler was elected in a democracy.

Some years later I attended a late-night editing session in northern Moscow. The editing rooms were in what was obviously a grand late-nineteenth-century mansion. Its state was decayed and dirty and it had a menace about it that made me feel uncomfortable. I enquired later about its history and was told that it had been the lair of Beria, the appalling bespectacled head of the NKVD, the former KGB, who used it for his not infrequent rape and murder sessions.

But let's get back to Rome and Mr Welles.

One morning in the Hotel Cipriani, Mr Welles told me to be there early with a microphone and recording equipment. When I arrived, I met a senior vice president from Young & Rubicam in New York, who were using Mr Welles for their television strapline 'United, the Wings of Man.'

Mr Welles sat forward and delivered the line once. Then, he looked challengingly at his terrified client, the advertising man, and said, 'How was that?'

'Good,' replied the New Yorker, 'but can we do just one more?'

'If it was good – and you said it, not me – why do you want to do another take?'

The executive mumbled something about safety. Mr Welles stood up and the recording was at an end.

Later that day, we invited the executive for lunch at Harry's Bar, the former haunt of Hemingway and other American expatriates, famous or rich, or both, such as Barbara Hutton and Cary Grant. It was Robert Benchley, that much-forgotten humourist, who penned the infamous telegram, 'Arrived Venice. Streets flooded. Please advise.'

★

'My doctor told me I had to stop throwing intimate dinners for four unless there are three other people.'

★

'We are going to Harry's for lunch,' Mr Welles announced. As we crossed the water on the hotel private launch, he talked about the legendary watering hole: 'During the '30s and '40s, lots of other bars in Venice that were not doing so well tried to infer it was a den of iniquity. Mussolini was in power, Italy was a police state, and the rumours spread that it was a secret hangout for homosexuals and conspiring Jews gathering there in defiance of the racist segregation laws.'

We stepped off the launch and headed into the narrow alley behind St Mark's Square by the opening of Grand Canal: 'You see, it is tucked away, a perfect place for secret meetings. In fact, the smear tactics actually attracted disreputable people like me, Peggy Guggenheim who was quite hedonist, Barbara Hutton, another desperate woman, Somerset Maugham and, of course, Hemingway. My God he could drink.'

Mr Welles pushed through the door of the famous bar: 'That's where he used to sit. He wrote all of *Across the River and into the Trees* right there. Giuseppe Cipriani told me that he used as much paper writing cheques out for his bills as he did on his novels.'

Harry's Bar has a relatively small dining room with a small, low bar rather than a restaurant, and tables arranged close to each other around the room. We sat down and ordered pasta, or at least Mr Welles ordered pasta, for all of us, telling us it was some of the best homemade pasta in all of Italy. He knew – being an authority on the subject – so we all looked forward to our meal.

He plucked another tale out of his gigantic mind, that bottomless mine of memories: 'Georges Braque sat at this very table and offered Giuseppe a painting in lieu of cash as payment. Giuseppe refused, saying, "I don't care if you don't have any money today, eat your fill and pay me when you do." What style! No wonder the man has had to sell out.'

The pasta came and the steaming plates were placed before us. The nervous waiter then began, without asking, to sprinkle parmigiano onto our plates. Suddenly Mr Welles let out a cross between a scream and a roar, like a great wounded buffalo. 'No! No! No! Not on my pasta! Never without asking the guest first! Take it away! In fact, take everything away. Take the waiter away. Take him away, out of my sight! I never want to see him again! He shouldn't be working in a place like this. Such an ignorant man!'

The maître d' rushed across and the other clientele, all of whom were already aware that Orson Welles was in the restaurant, cringed into their chairs and fell silent. It was as if the proverbial bomb had gone off. It had.

'What is the matter, Mr Welles?' pleaded the maître d.'

'What do you think? screamed Welles, 'Your ill-mannered waiter has put parmigiano on my pasta without first asking whether I wanted it.'

Mr Welles, breathing heavily now, grabbed a large wine glass and reached into his pocket. He struggled for a moment before pulling out a huge wad of $100 bills. He dramatically peeled one off the top, held it up for us all to see, as if it was one of his magic shows, struck a match and lit the money, letting it burn vigorously before dropping it into the glass to burn itself to cinders. 'That would have been yours if you'd given us better service,' he growled to the terrified waiter.

The waiter started to mumble apologies, but the maître d' hustled him away to some ghastly fate. Remember, this was Venice, the city of daggers, dark alleys and dangerous canals. The maître d' quickly returned and announced that lunch was on the house.

Mr Welles shrugged his shoulders like a spoilt child. 'Eat,' he said to us, and we nervously complied while he drank a whole glass of red wine down in one before I filled his glass again.

Charles Gray, suave as ever, braved the silence. 'And when, Orson, in the magic trick does the money get returned to the waiter?'

Mr Welles scoffed and smiled sheepishly.

He was soon served his replacement pasta and was even offered some parmigiano by the maître d.' He accepted, and was served a little. 'Too much parmigiano drowns the taste of the dish,' he announced, and we all agreed.

As we had coffee, he pulled out another $100 bill and held it in front of me.

'Put parmigiano on it, Dorian,' jested Charles.

I sat transfixed while the magician that was Mr Welles performed a sleight-of-hand conjuring trick for me. He tore the note in half then recovered it from my pocket. We all applauded. That huge man in black, moments before a howling monster, was now a beaming performer with delicate dexterous hands weaving their magic. At the end of the trick, he returned the dollar bill to me and told me to keep it.

I have thought about that incident many times since. The stories of Hollywood monsters are legion. Hideous demands for more money; non-payment of money owed; crazy demands; unreasonable requirements; actors who cannot be addressed except through third parties or who you're not allowed to look in the face. And that doesn't surprise me. When you pay men or women huge sums of money to ply their trade, sums of money that far exceed their needs, they will, in all likelihood, begin to get out of their prams.

From the vast sums of money paid to them they will deduce two things. First, that they can buy anything they want, and I mean anything, not just material things, but the important things like love or loyalty. What they forget is that those things have no price. Second, they begin to believe that they are worth these vast sums of money and that since they are worth more than mortal men they can behave like gods, dispensing benevolence or malevolence as they wish. Normal people are looked upon as ordinary, as opposed to extraordinary. They can be treated as inferior beings or *Untervolk*, as the Germans put it, since they are not part of the pantheon on Olympus.

Mr Welles, in this disturbing incident, behaved like one of those smug and self-obsessed Olympians. I don't blame him, it was just an unfortunate episode that disappointed me and made me sad. But my sadness didn't have to last long.

As we left Harry's Bar, Mr Welles took me aside. 'You know that $100 bill? Take it and give it to that poor bastard waiter.'

I looked shell-shocked. Mr Welles grabbed my shoulder and pushed me back into the restaurant. I went straight up to the maître d' and asked him where the waiter was.

'He's in the back. In the kitchens. He's very upset.'

So I followed him through the kitchen and out to the back. The waiter was sitting on a wine barrel, smoking and sobbing. It was a very Italian sight. I went straight up to him. 'Mr Welles is also upset,' I lied, 'and he wants you to have this.'

I pushed the dollar bill into his face and, at first, he shook his head. 'Come on, *prende lo*,' I insisted, '*e finite adesso*.'

He reluctantly took the note and nodded in thanks.

As I walked back through Harry's I asked the maître d' if the waiter's job was on the line. 'Mr Welles does not want that,' again I lied.

'No problem, he can stay with us. No problem.'

I walked out into the Piazza San Marco and saw Mr Welles standing there – a giant among the people and the pigeons. He was not such a bad guy after all. What did Acton say? 'Power tends to corrupt, and absolute power corrupts absolutely. Great men are almost always bad men.' Very true, but I would modify the second sentence. Great men are not always bad, but power, which they often wield, has a tendency to corrupt them and very often they become bad.

I never discovered what happened to the waiter at Harry's Bar.

A few evenings later, we were eating at the Trattoria alla Madonna. Mr Welles was in full flow, a glass of Friuli in one hand, his serviette tucked into his shirt collar to protect it from the black squid pasta sauce he was eating. He swigged a mouthful of wine, put his glass down and grabbed my hand: 'This hand that touches you now, Dorian, once touched the hand of Sarah Bernhardt. It did. Can you imagine that? And when she was young, Mademoiselle Bernhardt had taken the hand of Madame George, who had been the mistress of Napoleon! At this very moment in time you are three handshakes away from Napoleon! It's not that the world is so small, but that history is so short. Four or five very old men could join hands and take you right back to Shakespeare.'

I was suitably impressed to have been placed so close to one of my greatest heroes.

At that moment, I noticed a middle-aged couple, clearly Americans, had spotted Mr Welles from the other side of the restaurant. Cameras at the ready, they marched towards our table. I feared the worst, after the events at Harry's Bar. I froze, then got up to try to block them but it was too late. They brushed past me and asked if they could take a picture. We all waited for the explosion – which never came. Mr Welles was all sweetness and light and full of ingratiating smiles.

Our waiter in Harry's Bar had not been so lucky.

'We're from Iowa,' she told him. 'Can we take just one picture and I can tell my son? He's in Vietnam right now.'

'I would be honoured,' said Mr Welles, and he stood happily between them while I took the picture.

After thanking him politely they walked away and we were left alone.

'Vietnam, poor boy,' muttered Mr Welles.

'I'm glad she didn't put parmigiano on your pasta, Orson,' sniggered Charles.

By this time, Mr Welles was getting irritated by Charles Gray. The great man looked at me and raised his eyebrows in exasperation. Then he lost his temper, like a flash of lightning followed by thunder. He bellowed like a wounded buffalo, then smashed his fist down on the table. I was virtually lifted off my seat by the impact. 'Enough, Charles! Enough of your knavery. Put it away and let me not hear such dullardly snipes again.'

The trattoria fell silent. Charles fell silent, like a chastised schoolboy, and my heart started beating at an inordinate rate.

The storm passed and Mr Welles raised his glass. 'To future productions, to success and to parmigiano!'

'To parmigiano!' we all toasted and the waiters stared at us as if we were from another planet.

That evening, as we crossed the Grand Canal in a water taxi after dinner, Mr Welles and I stood outside in the cooling breeze while everyone else stayed inside. We stood next to each other, holding on to the varnished wooden roof and taking in that complicated aquatic avenue of palazzos sliding by on the Grand Canal.

'In years to come, when they ask you what Orson Welles taught you, tell them he was like a father to you and he taught you about Venice,' he said.

'Yes, I will,' I replied quietly, as the breeze made his cigar glow brighter in the darkness.

'I never had a son,' he pondered. 'The idea of the wisdom of the experienced being passed on to the young appeals to me. It is the way of most societies. In fact, the more primitive the society the more it manifests itself.'

The taxi chugged on across the open water. 'Learning is two things,' I suggested, invigorated by the Venetian prosecco. 'Firstly the watching and copying of things you think might work for you and secondly the actual accumulation of abilities, be they physical or mental.'

'Yes, boy, true enough. But most of all it is the acquiring of knowledge and its intelligent application that is true wisdom, a quality you find in few men. God knows, I am supposedly a wise man now. Or thousands of people think I am. But I am also a fool, a miscalculator, a man of many mistakes and …' He drew on his cigar again and shrugged his shoulders in helplessness, '… Many weaknesses. Jesus, I pursued that mad woman Lea for months. Months! Just to prove to myself that I could impose my will on her. And with Rita, God bless her, the sweetest woman in the world, I didn't have the guts to leave her before I did. She only married Ali because I didn't love her enough.'

'And Oja?' I asked.

He smiled with his cigar held by his teeth, slightly piratical. 'She fulfils my needs. No questions asked. No needs denied. She is wonderful.'

The wind was getting up now and the open water was choppy.

'Yes, I am trying to teach you about Venice. If you understand the complexities of Venice, you begin to understand life: its beauty which touches the souls of artists, its unpredictability, its mystery, its dark and secret alleys, its dingy canals, its decay and its past. Put all those together and you will have achieved much.'

That Orson Welles was an artist, there is no doubt.

And Venice, once visited, somehow, touches the souls of all who bear that cross.

29

The Black Pearl

Josephine Baker was intoxicating. The fact that I had partaken of one too many Bellinis at the plush bar of the Grand Hotel des Bains next door may have had something to do with it.

I had sauntered across to the Palazzo del Cinema on the Lido, past the hugely embarrassing gigantic poster of Oja that I had organised to be mounted in a provocative pose as a teaser for *The Deep*. It was the Venice Biennale, after all, and Mr Welles had either proposed it to promote the unfinished film, or to raise money for it to finish, or to appease a possibly frustrated Oja. Who knows? It was my job to labour and not seek any reward, save that of knowing that what he demanded he got.

To repeat, Josephine Baker, was intoxicating.

With her wavering voice, reminiscent of Billie Holliday records, and her uninhibited physically suggestive dancing, she was something special. She must have been well into her 60s by then and 60 in those days was a not-inconsiderable age. She had been brought up in poverty in St Louis, Missouri, a little like her follower, Eartha Kitt, who likewise seduced sophisticated Europe with her visceral and shameless use of her sensuousness and sexuality.

Her parents were both small-time performers and she was taken on stage from an early age. After becoming a chorus girl on Broadway and realising she could not get better than this in the US, she took a trip to France and never looked back. She was

19 years of age, it was 1925, and she was an immediate hit in Paris with her exotic and suggestive dances.

She became a French citizen, supported the Resistance during the war and was awarded the Croix de Guerre, the Rosette de la Résistance and the Légion d'Honneur. She lived in a château in the Dordogne where she raised orphaned children. The year before I saw her, Coretta King had even approached her to lead the Civil Rights Movement following the assassination of her husband. All in all, she was a remarkable woman and a great performer, although Mr Welles was not that keen:

> No, not for me. You guys go and enjoy the show. I've seen her in Paris. Give me Eartha any day. She was the one for me: the most exciting woman in the world. More sexy than Josephine, more sexy than anyone I've ever known.

In Venice, accompanied by a full orchestra, Josephine, the 'Black Pearl,' did all her old dance routines, including 'Danse Sauvage,' a kind of Carmen Miranda number with a lot of bumping and grinding. Then she sang her big hit 'J'ai deux amours,' which brought the house down and a number of other French hits of the time, such as the Françoise Hardy number, 'Tous les Garçons et les Filles,' and Edith Piaf's 'Non, Je ne Regrette Rien,' which again caused a big stir in the audience.

This was particularly poignant, since this heroine of so many things was now virtually destitute and was singing for her supper. Just a few months before, her beautiful château had been repossessed by the financial authorities and she was homeless.

Our work was virtually done in Venice, and as we drove home to Asolo in my little car, I realised that the brief interlude with Mr Welles and these very English actors had been fun in a beautiful place.

Two years later, watching Visconti's *Death in Venice* in a cinema near Baker Street and listening to the monumentally moving Mahler music, I thought back on those times in La Serenissima, where the lightness of touch of the company I had kept lifted my spirits in that dark damp city.

The next morning, Mr Welles summoned me and secretly told me to pay off the crew since he wanted to leave the next day to go to Vienna. I was to return with the equipment to Rome. It was as if he was bored, or maybe the money had run out.

★

'I sat next to Hitler once in Innsbruck. I was a youth on a walking tour with one of my teachers from school. It was a very fashionable thing to do in those days.'

'Yes, my father did it, walking in Bavaria and the Tyrol. He used to sing all the German marching songs, which unfortunately had a more sinister connotation after 1945.'

'Exactly,' said Mr Welles. 'Anyway, my teacher was a proto-Fascist and took me to a Nazi rally. They were just a joke then at the beginning of the 1930s. The ghastly Julius Streicher was there shouting a lot. God, he was ugly! Then we went for a beer in one of those Austrian bierkellers, and on the bench I found myself next to a characterless man who just stared straight ahead of him and watched the proceedings. He didn't drink, you know, and never even looked at me. It was definitely him, with the brushed forward hair and the trim moustache. Extraordinary that, in front of a crowd, he could become a screaming maniac powered by hatred.'

I echoed his story with my own, more recent one. In Munich on the way down to Italy I had spent an evening in a Bavarian bierkeller with my friend Steve Shane. Much beer was consumed, which triggered constant return visits to the urinals, part of the punishment for drinking beer. Sitting down again, I noticed a pasty-faced individual in his mid-70s quietly drinking on his own. His skin was almost ceramic in texture and he had a grey moustache and grey hair brushed at an angle across his forehead.

It was Adolf Hitler, without a doubt. I pointed this out to Steve who quickly agreed. The man drank metronomically and systematically, as Hitler would. But then I remembered that Hitler was a teetotaller.

'No matter,' said Steve, 'it's part of his disguise.'

'So Hitler is alive and well and living in Munich, the city of his first triumphs?'

'Exactly,' replied Steve.

'It was the same man,' agreed Mr Welles.

★

Asolo appealed to all one's aesthetic senses. But for me the icing on the cake was one afternoon when we walked into the empty hotel restaurant. There, sitting in a discreet corner far from prying eyes, were Faye Dunaway and her lover Marcello Mastroainni. That time they were two of the most famous stars in the world, with her having beguiled us all in *Bonnie and Clyde* and he, Fellini's male muse. He was the quintessential Latin lover – black-haired, brown-eyed and very handsome – while she was exquisitely chiselled and remote.

Mr Welles wandered over to them and was warmly embraced by the Mastroianni. I stood nervously by before Mr Welles introduced me to them both. He was easy and warm, she restrained and distant, an 'ice queen' if ever there was one, or a '60s Garbo. As I leaned forward to speak to her, I detected the aroma of her scent: clean and clear like water from a mountain stream. She was in awe of Mr Welles and almost girlish in his presence.

As we walked away after the pleasantries, Mr Welles muttered to me: 'He will break her heart. He will never leave his wife. Italians never do. And beneath her ice-cool exterior there lurks a vulnerable creature.'

30

The Parting of Ways

It was the beginning of autumn and the gentle signs of a Mediterranean winter had begun to appear, with the occasional evening when it was too cold to eat outside in Rome's endless piazzas. There were fewer diners at the 'Othello' trattoria and I could easily get a table for one.

I picked up Mr Welles every day in the Mini and drove back to Fono Roma, where we would go to continue fiddling with *The Deep*. And fiddling he was: making endless miniscule changes, running and rerunning sequences, with just the noise of his breathing in the darkened and cigar-smelling editing room to signal his dissatisfaction, or at least uncertainty about another particular sequence – often the same sequence we had changed days before. The truth is, he was uncertain as to the quality of the material, both in terms of the performances and technically. He was fiddling while Rome burned.

Even on Sundays we would go there. I persuaded the janitor of the building to give me a key and we would enter the building by a back entrance, go downstairs through the basement and then up into the cutting room. It was a reclusive existence. And we were getting nowhere.

I got the feeling we were under mental siege and we were not going to win. I was too naïve to understand that he had virtually run out of money. All telephone calls were refused – for example, one from Roman Polanski – so I felt cut off from the outside world.

One day, with Mr Welles clearly in a black mood, I was accused of reluctance to work with some derisory words on the telephone. Furthermore, I heard Oja in the background urging him on to chastise his slave. I took offence and retired to my hotel and sulked, hurt that he had accused me, one of his most loyal subjects, of being workshy.

I had noted this tendency between Mr Welles and Oja for a while now, when talking about others, and I did not want to be included in this suspicion syndrome. It was like an old king listening to just the words he wanted to hear from his court favourite. I worked hard and loyally for him, and I had had enough.

We were going nowhere, so after a day of soul-searching I composed a short note to him.

Dear Mr Welles,

I was distressed to note the tone of suspicion in our conversation today. As you know I work hard and honestly for you. For some time now, I have felt somewhat frustrated by how things are going for me. You are a large tree which casts a great shadow on all those who are around you. I am a young sapling and I need the sun to let me grow.

Reluctantly, I think it is time for me to transplant myself.

I thank you for all you have done for me during this past year.

I will not forget any of it.

Dorian.

I took my note round to his hotel and gave it to the concierge. I then drove over to the Janicolo Hill which looks down across the cupolas and domes of Rome with St Peter's and the Castel San Angelo in the near distance. Behind me were the terracotta-coloured buildings where Garibaldi and his Redshirts had fought so bravely, but in vain, to halt the invading French Army summoned by Pio Nono to drive them from the walls of Rome and delay the course of Italian independence by a single decade.

I wondered what I would do, knowing that I had already finished my time with Mr Welles. I have thought about these moments often since. I had been living in a fascinating but closed world which seemed to have few pathways to the main-streams of my ambition. I was not on any particular career path and time was passing.

Sure, Mr Welles had directed *Citizen Kane* at the age of 24, so he, of all people, should have understood. When I returned to my little hotel there was a note for me, written in his scrawl:

Dear Dorian,

　I am sorry about how I spoke to you today. I may have used some unnecessarily harsh words. Perhaps you are right what you say. Why don't we discuss your position and improve the situation.

　Orson W.

Maybe he had been under pressure when he snapped at me earlier that day. Maybe he had had a falling out with Oja. But now he had rethought his opinion of me, maybe encouraged by Oja, with whom I had always got along. Anyway, it was big of him to have apologised and I was moved.

But the situation remained the same for me. I knew it would, in my heart, and I knew that tigers only rarely changed their stripes. To paraphrase Winston Churchill, 'same tiger, same stripes.'

Orson Welles had drunk from the chalice of success early, so why couldn't I? What I didn't appreciate was that his story had been different, and his circumstances were different. And anyway, what was I going to be able to put on my resume? He had talked a little about a Claude Chabrol movie we were going to do, where we would live in a house in the French countryside in the autumn. The thought of being enclosed again in this high-pressure and personal world did not fill me with joy.

I rang Ann Rogers in London and told her that, with sadness in my heart, I was going to leave.

'Why?' she enquired, but when I gave her my rather non-specific reasons, she seemed to understand. 'Maybe it's the right decision for you,' she said, and I told her that when I returned to London I would call her to resolve any details that needed tidying up.

The phone went back on its cradle and I rolled back onto the bed and stared at the faded cream ceiling of the room that had been my home for these past months. What was I going to do? Where was I going to go? I would think about it, but at least I wouldn't have to contend with the massive pressure that somehow Mr Welles managed to exert on all around him. Continually being tested, continually not knowing where we were going or what we were going to do, continually on the move, continually avoiding, continually evading, like being part of an upmarket gypsy band, moving from caravanserai to caravanserai.

I suppose he had always been like that: travelling on a ship across the Pacific to Shanghai when just a boy with his father; venturing to Ireland when still a teenager, although a large one, I suspect, and riding a donkey cart around the west coast of the Emerald Isle, paying his way in the cottages where he stayed by giving them paintings he was doing (are those paintings by Mr Welles still hanging, dusty, on those whitewashed stone walls?); walking into the Abbey Theatre in Dublin and telling Micheál Mac Liammóir that he was a well-known New York actor and getting away with it; the Mercury Theatre, the *Mercury Theatre on the Air* and the invasion from Mars tricking the city of New York; the introduction and immersion in film-making, like a duck to water; instant, and almost too easy success and adulation so long ago.

Was he hurt by Rita Hayworth leaving him for the perennial universal playboy Ali Khan? Did he leave America because there was nothing for him there? How could that be? Surely there must have been producers who could handle this renegade, who did wonderful things on screen? I could never believe there was not one person in all of Hollywood who did not have the courage, intellect, arrogance, greed, ego or nous to handle Orson Welles.

Apparently not, although they are telling us, to this day, how daring they are, how smart they are, how perceptive they are. Was Orson Welles too complicated for all of them?

Maybe.

31

REFLECTIONS ON CASSIUS MARCELLUS CLAY

Back in that hotel room, I decided I needed a break from all these thoughts. So, I checked out of the hotel and drove down to Naples.

Rome was small and claustrophobic, particularly in my tiny hotel room. Naples was big, open and different. I walked along that splendidly faded esplanade and wandered through the narrow washing-flagged side streets. I took a ferry over to Capri and wandered its tourist-free lanes, swam in the limpid emerald green Mediterranean and glanced up the cliffs to where the debauched Emperor Tiberius had bathed in the sun with his 'minnow' boy attendants, while Peter and Paul and the other early followers of the renegade rabbi Joshua, from Nazareth in Judaea, spread the word across his Eastern Empire.

As the ferry took me back across the majestic Bay of Naples, I remembered those days with Mr Welles in Caserta as I sat in his dressing room and watched him apply yet another of the hapless fake noses he was so fond of. 'I've got a baby face. So, I have to give myself some character, some difference. It's my theatre background, nothing to do with the movies.' The only trouble was those endless noses looked so fake, so amateur. Better the real Mr Welles.

Had he really been a war correspondent landing in Naples during the Italian campaign? How on earth did he have time? He always felt as though he should have taken some part in the war. 'I was never a soldier. Look at me. I failed the medicals over and over. Are you surprised? Unlike Dr Johnson, I think I would have chosen the company of Socrates rather than that of Charles XII.'

What was he up to during the war years after *Kane*? His meetings with President Roosevelt in the White House – Orson Welles and Franklin Roosevelt together, talking of what, I wondered? I wonder even now.

The Ambassador of Goodwill and *It's All True*, the unfinished film in Brazil on the carnival, full of masks and mystery, its footage never cut and never used. The awful tale of how he had sent the Brazilian fisherman, Jacare, to his death.

Arriving in Brazil and looking for local material, he had heard the story of the four fishermen from Fortaleza who, wishing to protest to the President of Brazil about their working conditions, had sailed from the tropical seas of the north of Brazil the 1,600 miles down to Rio de Janeiro in what was little more than a raft with a sail. The president granted them their wishes and they became national heroes.

Mr Welles approached them and persuaded them to re-enact some of their experiences. They put out to sea and immediately Jacare realised it was too rough. He turned back twice, but twice Mr Welles offered him more money and twice the desperately poor man agreed. Minutes later, a big wave hit them and Jacare was washed away, never to be seen again. His head was found in the belly of a shark some months later.

Mr Welles became a pariah overnight in Brazil. He was forced to flee. 'God forbid, I was not trying to drown him. I miscalculated, but my name was dirt after that. The studio pulled the money and as I left the hotel I was spat at in the street.'

Power had already corrupted him, and he was incapable of seeing his error. Again, the painter in his studio with extreme ideas, and unpaintable canvases. Shooting with no script, risking too much.

Finally, he was cast with Charlton Heston, his friend Chuck, in *Touch of Evil*, who persuaded the studio to let him direct another dark masterpiece.

Then, twenty years in Europe and Ropama Films – Rome, Paris, Madrid, his triumvirate of cities. Forever in search of money, forever questioned about the past and why it was so clever and so good. And again, why no volunteers to produce for him, to finance him, to let him do the things he wanted to do? The things he did do, like *Othello* and *Chimes at Midnight*, were wonderful and imaginative without any money or support, so how much more could he have done with proper backing? So many unanswered questions.

What heinous crime had he done to merit the sneers, the sighs of regret, the 'might have beens,' the 'it's a pity,' the 'what's he done recently?' Still a mystery, like the man himself, with his magic tricks, as if he really were Harry Lime, the man in the shadows, dressed like the fin de siècle absinthe drinkers in the Pernod posters, drinking bottles of cognac hard when acting in his cameo roles and hating them, and forever suggesting angles and cuts to lesser directors than he.

His giant inventive intelligence was hardly ever released in controlled or ordered fashion within a controlled or ordered financial framework. Maybe it wasn't all those others. Maybe it was just him, sensitive and intelligent enough to truly judge the limitations of his own abilities, afraid to approach those dangerous borders for fear of witnessing his own shortcomings. So just try another canvas, daub some more paint, and don't take that road that only leads to self-judgement and disappointment; just look down its winding way and turn away because when you follow its path it only leads to frustration and not fulfilment.

To all the world, he had stood on the mountain top, and he knew that people who had breathed that rarefied air never returned, and, if they tried, were in mortal danger of falling. Few artists climb Everest twice.

Heroes are there for us to astonish at, to marvel at, to be disappointed by, to despise, to bring back down to our mortal level, somehow to aspire to, but at the same time to want to destroy, as if anything out of the 'norm' was a sin – the pack wanting to bring the wanderers back into line.

In the 1960 Olympics I had witnessed, on a flickering black and white television set, images transmitted in this same city, another young hero, a lithe young man from Louisville, Kentucky. Cassius Marcellus Clay won a gold medal in the light-heavyweight division of boxing. And, despite my dour obedience to false modesty, I had been spellbound by his naked braggadocio and dazzling athleticism.

The world quickly formed two camps – those on his side, smiling with him and his wit, and the vast majority, who wanted to see his fall. In boxing, it was a literal fall. He took the world on a rollercoaster ride. Those of us who loved him gloried in his triumphs, his just victories over the brutish thugs he shared the ring with, his torrent of witty, perceptive lines almost classic in their ability to parody serious literature. 'I float like a butterfly and sting like a bee, Muhammad Ali,' his gladiatorial challenges to one and all. His courageous stand, which he need not have made, on Vietnam with its awful three-year ban taking away probably his three best years as an athlete. His brave return and poignant defeat by the savage warrior, Joe Frazier. We all feared for him in Zaire, and again he surprised us in what was probably his greatest and most unlikely triumph.

In Manila in 1976 I met the man who had refereed that fight and he confirmed to me what I had first read in Norman Mailer's *The Fight*, that when he drew the two protagonists together Ali had stared down Foreman and whispered to him, before the unknowing crowd, that he had been reading about him since he was a boy, that he was a legend and now he was in the ring with that legend and the legend would inevitably defeat him.

Then the Manila fight, with Frazier boring forward relentlessly, round after round, brutally bludgeoning our hero; the bludgeon against the rapier of Ali's jab, and finally that instant when Frazier faltered just an inch, going back rather than forward, and I knew it was another victory, albeit pyrrhic.

Then the slow decline of all athletes as they attempt things their minds think they can achieve but to which their bodies cannot respond. In recent years, when I think of that night in the hotel room, I tend to think of Ali and that sad epilogue at Atlanta in 1996 as he stumbled bravely into the stadium, fired the arrow with his shaking hands and lit the Olympic flame before the whole world, and we all remembered and wept.

I drove north out of Naples past Rome and headed across Tuscany, Emilia and Lombardy, past Lake Maggiore and up into the Alps towards Switzerland. I had walked away from what was an impossible situation, with no advantage to myself except my memories of that unfathomable man called Orson Welles. A man who had extraordinarily foretold his own future in the first film he ever made, with Charles Foster Kane hopelessly trying to make his second wife, Susan, into an opera star, like William Randolph Hearst trying to make his mistress, Marion Davies, into a serious actress, and now Orson Welles himself trying and failing to create a career for his mistress, Oja.

I had betrayed him, but saved myself from being dragged down in that vortex which he would inevitably create as he upended and plunged slowly into the gloomy depths of that unknown ocean we call the afterlife, leaving just the flotsam and jetsam of ill-thought-out projects, half-written scripts, and partially delivered soliloquies from parts he longed to play and never did.

To say any of his latter efforts were profound is just plain ludicrous. There is just one voiceover on a rather inadequate shot of France's Chartres Cathedral that reaches towards profundity. It grew from a conversation we once had on the Lido in Venice, when I suggested to him that the only relics of 2,000 years of European history would be those magnificent medieval cathedrals lying like great beached battleships across the horizons of Europe, monolithic, silent, majestic and powerful, dwarfing the cities that cluster around them and the countryside beyond. Future travellers will witness them and be amazed as we of these times stand in awe at the pyramids and the ruins of ancient Greece and Rome, built by previous generations of man.

His text reads as follows:

Now this has been standing here for centuries the premier work of man perhaps in the whole Western world and it's without a signature, Chartres. A celebration to God's glory and to the dignity of man, while all that's left most artists seem to feel these days is man, naked, poor, forked, ratish. There aren't any celebrations.

Ours, the scientists keep telling us, is a universe which is disposable.

You know, it might be just this one anonymous glory, of all things, this rich stone forest, this epic chant, this gaiety, this grand choiring shout of affirmation which we choose, when all our cities are dust, to stand intact, to mark where we have been, to testify to what we had it in us to accomplish.

Our works in stone, in paint, in print are spared, some of them for a few decades or a millennium or two but everything must finally fall in awe or [wear] away into the ultimate and universal ash, the triumph and the frauds, the treasures and the fakes, a fact of life.

We are going to die.

'Be of good heart!' cry the dead artists out of the living past. 'Our songs will all be silenced but what of it?'

Go on singing. Maybe a man's name doesn't matter that much.

Whenever I listen to it, I hear the almost Shakespearian iambic pentameter in the writing and delivery and it always reminds me somehow of John of Gaunt's dying speech in *Richard II*. It is a wonderful piece of poetic prose.

I remember after that conversation, as we took the water taxi back to the Grand Canal, we sat outside in the warm evening breeze and over the engine noise Mr Welles shouted, 'It's all about the doing that's important. Looking to posterity is a pastime for vain men. Just be and do and history will take care of the rest.'

His cigar, buffeted by the breeze, was making too many sparks in the darkening light, so he cast it away beyond the wake of the boat and I watched it disappear in the distance.

'There are so many myths about me, I can't even remember which is true and which is myth. I'll take them both for the moment. I was in Vienna for just a few days to do The Third Man. *And the whole world thinks I wrote it, directed it and starred in it. I did star in it, but just for a few fleeting moments. But I did find the zither player and introduced him to Carol. Carol was a good director. The idea that he copied my style is horse-shit.'*

32

A Close-Run Thing

I saw Ann Rogers one more time.

It was some months later, and I had travelled to Munich to meet a New York-based television producer about a script based on the story of Byron and Shelley and their adventures in Switzerland and Italy. He had told me on the telephone that maybe he could help me advance the project.

When I arrived at Munich Airport, the executive met me with a male American friend. The executive only had eyes for me and his greeting as I was exiting arrivals was much too friendly. He was slight of build and reminded me somewhat of the Young & Rubicam vice president with who I had dealt with in Venice with Mr Welles, but it was not he.

His friend, who greeted me with an over-enthusiastic, 'Hello Dorian, I've heard so much about you!' was most unattractive with a huge belly, fat legs bulging inside tight filthy jeans and a t-shirt too small for him. He had a pathetic attempt at a moustache, thinning lank hair, small eyes and a nose too big for his face. In a word, he was hideous: worse still, lechery lurked beneath. These were the days before the internet, but I dread to think what sort of material he would have excited himself with in this day and age.

I realised as we walked to the car that both of them were sexual predators and I was fair game. Of course, I stupidly realised, the diminutive executive probably perceived that Byron and Shelley, in their big shirts and Regency tight trousers, were of his persuasion as well. I was trying to make a film on the subject, so he would have assumed I had the same tastes as well. I cursed myself for not realising this before, and for walking into his trap. But I had to be polite since he was an indirect friend of the family. My pathetic suggestion that I go to my hotel fell on deaf ears and was politely overruled by both my companions, who insisted I stay with them; it would be cheaper for me and there was space.

Once in Ugly's dingy apartment, I realised there was only one bedroom, where I nervously put my overnight case. I drew a deep breath and went back into the sitting room. I was offered a drink, which I refused, and we chatted for a while before heading out to dinner at a fancy hotel restaurant. Talk about an elephant in the room, this one was a hairy mammoth with gigantic tusks.

At dinner I again refused a drink, saying that I was a teetotaller, which was far from the truth. I felt I had to keep my wits about me. We had a pleasant enough meal before returning to the flat, where I had a horrible feeling he planned to carry out the dirty deed, aided and abetted by his sidekick, who was probably going to watch.

Ridiculously, I turned in for bed while they drank brandy in the adjoining room. I put on my pyjamas, as all good boys do, and got into bed and switched out the lamp. My heart was beating loudly and my mouth was dry with terror.

After a short while, the executive came into the room and also undressed and got into bed. Whether he was wearing his pyjamas or was completely naked, I will never know. Picture this ridiculous scene, with me lying there in the darkness in total silence pretending to be asleep, waiting for the groping hand to slide across onto my thigh and for me to politely remove it.

But it never happened.

Because, like Mr Welles at his glittering dinner party with Mr Goldwyn and Mr Mayer, when he forgot his punchline, I was saved by an Act of God.

I suddenly, and without any warning, vomited dreadfully. And in the Olympic Games of vomiting, this was right up there in gold medal position. I vomited and vomited, loudly and aggressively. I had no idea there was so much content in my stomach.

The executive leapt out of bed in horror and ran to get a bucket, a bowl, anything to take my excretions. I was retching helplessly now, drenched in sweat, and dry retching when there was no more liquid in my body. I thought I was going to die.

The executive and Ugly were running about the flat throwing towels and containers at me as I mumbled apologies between more regurgitations. They called the ambulance, which in true German style, arrived promptly. The only problem was the ambulance men were enormous in their winter coats and the flat was tiny.

My limp body was strapped onto a stretcher so effectively that I was pinned. My head lolled onto my chest and I had no strength in my body. I was like a hand puppet without the hand, so I never saw the ambulance men roll their eyes at me in disapproval, assuming I had been indulging in a homosexual threesome. In any event, in my semi-conscious state I didn't care. They were taking me to safety.

The lift of the apartment block was so tiny that they could not fit me in without raising the stretcher into a vertical position. So, there I was pinned to this board, my arms strapped at my sides, the light of the lift blazing into my eyes, my head throbbing as a result, as though it was going to explode, with these two gigantic ambulance men, neither of whom spoke a word of English. I faded in unconsciousness.

At Munich General Hospital I was swiftly wheeled into an equally bright operating theatre where a group of doctors gathered round me and proceeded to force a rubber pipe down my throat and give me a stomach pump, although I can't believe there was anything in there to pump out. Anyway, we all know the Germans are nothing if not thorough. Sweating heavily and choking on the rubber pipe in my throat I thrashed around on the operating table like a freshly landed fish. Eventually an older doctor peered down at me and told me I had food poisoning and that I could have died.

'We are putting you on a drip immediately to build up your body fluids and in a few days you should be OK.'

'A few days,' I gurgled.

The doctor ignored me as he stabbed the catheter into my arm for the intravenous pipe. The pain made me focus, although my instinct was to go to sleep despite the glaring lights. 'What did you eat?' he enquired.

In my vagary I tried to remember, then I got it.

'Smoked eel. At the Munich Hotel.'

'Very nice. The Munich Hotel, I mean. The eel must have been off. That kind of food poisoning can be very dangerous. You are lucky.'

'You don't know how lucky,' I thought to myself.

I was wheeled out of the operating theatre and into a long dark corridor. It was the middle of winter in Germany and outside the windows it was black. I was left on the trolley as the last nurse walked away down the corridor. I lay there listening, my head still throbbing but the nausea gone. I was too exhausted to move, but at the same time mentally alert. It was a strange feeling, a disturbing feeling, almost as if I had been administered a drug to weaken my body but not my mind.

All through the long night I lay there, wondering what I was going to do next. All I could hear were the occasional groans of men in the nearby wards. Even the thought that I had escaped the clutches of the two predators didn't make me feel any better. But I had, and it was good.

As dawn broke and some lights were switched on, I was wheeled into a ward and put into bed. Miraculously my shoes, clothes and overnight bag were in a locker next to the bed. God knows how they got there. The ward was something else. All the patients were dressed in grey pyjamas or dressing gowns, some had bandages round their heads, others had slings on their arms and they seemed to move very slowly. They spoke in whispers and hardly looked at me.

It was as though I was in this self-same hospital in December 1942 and I was one of the lucky *Wehrmacht* soldiers who had been wounded at Stalingrad and evacuated to Germany. Some of their wounds seemed pretty severe to me, particularly the ones that just lay in their beds not moving.

As the nurses, also in grey, came round, they looked at my notes and spoke to me in German.

'*Ich bin ein Englander*,' I ventured, in my best Second World War German, '*nein sprechen Deutsche*.'

'OK,' said the clearly capable nurse, 'You will have to stay here for at least a week to recover your strength. You should be dead now.' The Germans are not famous for their hyperbole.

She placed a bowl of what looked like porridge on the tray over my bed and walked away. I was certainly not going to eat it. Food at that moment, despite the fact that I was ravenously hungry, was not high on my agenda.

For the next three hours I lay there, weak with dehydration but with a brain that was working overtime. Finally, I decided on a course of action. I discreetly pulled the drip out of my arm and swung my legs over the side of the bed. The physical effort of doing this exhausted me and I sat there for a good ten minutes, not moving. One thing was for sure. I was not going be just another of these Stalingrad survivors. I was going to go back to the Front. I surreptitiously slipped slowly into my clothes and was just lacing up my boots when the head nurse arrived. In true medical style, she placed her hands on her hips in exasperation.

'What are you doing, sir?'

I froze in terror. I was in a German hospital. And this woman was straight out of a Leni Riefenstahl documentary on women athletes. She might even have performed at the Berlin Olympics in 1936 in front of Hitler. She was the right age.

'I am leaving. I have to leave. I have to be somewhere,' I said lamely.

'You are going nowhere, young man. You must stay here until the doctors examine you. I am off duty now but you will have to wait until they do their rounds this evening.'

For me, instilled with Second World War stories, this was like a scene from the hospital wing of a German prisoner-of-war camp, Stalag Luft IV-B maybe. I was now, in my mind, an RAF bomber pilot like my father and had been shot down after a raid over Düsseldorf.

The formidable nurse strode away, not realising she had made a mistake. She had given me a time window and I was not going to spend another night in that prison camp. I just waited and, in my mind, knotted my sheets together into an escape rope.

After waiting a while, I finished up lacing my shoes, picked up my bag and walked slowly out of the ward. I shuffled slowly down one of the endless corridors and finally found the reception of the enormous hospital and just slowly walked out. I couldn't walk fast. I didn't have the energy. I walked up to the taxi rank, opened the door and slid into the seat.

I asked to go to the railway station, from where I telephoned Anna Rogers in Innsbruck to tell her I was coming to see her. I had wanted to talk to her one more time about Mr Welles. I boarded the train in a third-class carriage which just had wooden benches. It was an uncomfortable three-hour ride, where again my body was exhausted but my mind alert, so I couldn't even fall asleep, which would have been impossible anyway on those hard, wooden benches. I still felt as if I was escaping from somewhere, and only relaxed when we crossed the Austrian border.

I stayed the night in Innsbruck and the next morning I went up into the mountains to Igls, where Ann Rogers was staying. I spent three days there, walking in the snow and recuperating.

'Mr Welles was very fond of you, you know.'

'And I was of him, more than fond. I loved him.'

'Yes, so do many of us, though sometimes I don't think he realises.'

'It's as if he's a great liner sweeping across the ocean, unable to alter course but followed by smaller ships who often travel slower but endeavour to keep up with him and the marvellous energy of his imagination.'

'That's very nicely put, young man, and I entirely understand you.'

We looked at the great ridge of mountains on the horizon, still high up in the sun while the valley below was sinking into darkness. They were massive and seemingly immovable, like sleeping giants.

'I just hope that great ship doesn't run aground one stormy night.'

'Well, Dorian, we all run aground one day. We just take what is given to us as our daily bread. And he has had more than most men.'

We walked on in silence in the blanket of snow, our boots crunching on the path as if we were walking on meringues. The afternoon sun dipped behind the fir trees, only narrow beams now illuminating our way.

'We'd better go in now and have a hot chocolate or something. What more can we say?'

Mr Rogers appeared at the doorway of the hotel. 'Come on, you Poms. I'm trying to watch the cricket from Sydney. You can't still be talking about that man?'

We were, and we always would. He had cast a giant shadow on our lives which still hangs across me now, decades later. But it is a good shadow, a shadow of light – which is a contradiction in terms, but I understand what it means.

As I kicked the snow off my boots, I smiled at the thought of trying to explain the machinations of cricket to Mr Welles. It was one of the few matters he knew precisely nothing about. Doubtless, given more time I could have taught him and in his prime he would have made a formidable fast bowler and a belligerent batsman, a sort of W.G. Grace, both in character and in looks.

33

African Perspective

'Africa, decades later,' the title should read.

Looking back on things with the advantage of perspective is the only way we can perceive things past. But memories are fickle companions, moving rapidly in and out of focus, selecting at random and then deselecting. And we stumble from one to the next without chapter endings or beginnings, without noticing where one becomes the other except when there are cataclysmic events such as deaths or partings, which mark significant punctuation in our lives. Otherwise, it is seamless.

The past is another country, for sure.

I am in Africa. Another country, for all mankind, somehow bestowing on me a sense of eternity.

★

'My time in Africa made me realise how insignificant and temporary we really are. The sheer scale of it dwarfs us as much as the great plains of America must have dwarfed the early settlers as they trekked westwards towards the distant Rockies not knowing what lay beyond.'

★

The oldest and most uncomplicated continent, unspoilt by man, however hard he tries, and almost unchanged from its original form. It's so big and so under-populated that problems of over-crowding and pollution don't yet apply. The skies are endless and huge, making you constantly aware of them.

There is little else to look at.

Man has hardly made his mark; he's only been around 100,000 years after making those little footprints in the Great Rift Valley, while Africa has been here 6 million years. So the continent existed about 5,900,000 years with just the sky for company. And it's good company, never dull, always varying in texture and colour, never to be ignored. I was right about the sky in Mr Welles' *Don Quixote*.

★

'I'm a bit of an outsider in this day and age. I would have been more accepted in past centuries where audiences were more used to men like me!'

★

The horizons stretch away north, south – in fact, in any direction you want your imagination to follow. And the whole feeling is of a primeval emptiness, with man and his manoeuvrings just touching the periphery of the planet, like dust on a deserted street, making no serious inroad into nature, which is peerless, all-powerful and endless.

And Africans accept…

A rich baritone voice echoed across the desert I was gazing at like the narrator of a documentary:

How on earth have they decided that Man started in Africa? They've just found a few bones in the Rift Valley, for God's sake. What if they find some other bones in the Mongolian

Desert? Or in Patagonia? Which they undoubtedly will. These so-called 'experts' are just guessing. They are as much in the dark as we are.

I'll give you an example. In 1938 a fish was discovered off the eastern coast of Southern Africa. It was called the coelacanth. Experts had decreed it to be extinct 65 million years ago. So, they were 65 million years wrong!

This pronouncement was followed by a stifled guffaw.

They accept their lot, the lot of man to suffer at the hands of the elements, nature, disease and the danger of other mammals more powerful than them. Contrary to preconceived historic notions continuing up to the present day in Europe and America and Asia, Africans are not lazy or less intelligent or less clean than their white cousins. Quite the reverse.

I never cease to be astonished at their ability to work endlessly for their own survival with precious little encouragement from nature, or their leaders, whose main ambition is to take as much as they can from their starving subjects.

So, Africa is as pure as any place on earth. Its people are trusting and believing. Its physical attributes – its savannah, mountains, jungles and deserts – are largely unblemished so far.

I am in one of these desert lands and I am remembering a time when I was surrounded by elaborate, intricate and complicated, but beautiful, man-made architecture, like the pencil and chalk drawings of Raphael, the mathematical harmonies of Johan Sebastian Bach, the sheer beauty of Mozart, the melodies of Puccini. Somehow, the purity and simplicity of where I sit makes it a little easier to handle memory.

★

'Looking to posterity is a ridiculous ambition.'

★

I am gazing across open bush country to some gently rolling hills to the west. The sun is plummeting swiftly behind the sharply depicted contours, which darken menacingly against the red-gold screen of the sky. The red-gold fades to a washed pink. It dims and fades to deep blue, penetrated by bright perforating stars making their mark for ancient bushmen navigators who wandered these inland seas centuries before I gazed upon them.

The same stars that Vasco da Gama had watched through his brass sextants, with black eyes shining in the night as he peered constantly shoreward to the Skeleton Coast, so beloved by Mr Welles in the film we had worked on together, trying to discern far-off white lines of surf crashing onto endless diamond-strewn beaches, dangerous to him and his brave band of brothers with only the sound of creaking wood and straining rope to hide the distant roar that was there and then was not.

A little touch of Orson Welles in the night.

★

'If you want a happy ending, it depends, of course, on where you stop your story.'

34

THE END GAME

Then came the end game.

On 10 October 1985, Welles appeared on *The Merv Griffin Show*, in what would be his last public appearance before his death. It was made all the more poignant by the personal, wistful turn taken by the discussion. Dressed in a navy-blue jacket with a sky-blue shirt and an ascot, Welles said that not long ago he'd begun thinking he was 70, when he was really only 69, meaning that he'd given himself an extra year. He told Griffin that he experienced 'certain parts of every day that are joyous,' continuing, 'I'm not essentially a happy person, but I have all kinds of joy.' On the difference between the two, he said, 'Joy is a great big electrical experience, but happiness is … a warthog can be happy.'

A few hours later, he died in the night, slumped over his typewriter, after a heart attack. He'd been working on a script for one of his crammed schedule of projects. It was a script for a TV show tentatively titled *Orson Welles Solo*.

His great heart had finally given out as he struggled bravely to fight the good fight, conveying ideas on paper and converting them into celluloid. What better way to die as a scriptwriter and storyteller, with his hands still on the keys, his head resting next to them as though thinking of one more idea. One more great idea that would finally set him free from his struggles and release him into the open country of stress-free creativity, with its horizons and possibilities far ahead.

On that water taxi in Venice as we crossed the open water to the Giudecca with the lights of the island flickering in the distance, he had said to me, 'There are men, Dorian, born into this world with a gaze fixed on the widest possible horizon. Men who can see without strain beyond the furthest distances into that unconquered country we call the future. Be one of those men and I will give you my blessing.' Then he threw his ailing cigar into the water and it fizzed, died, and was carried away in the the wash of the water taxi.

'I'll tell you another thing, Dorian. Don't ever give people what you think they want. Give them what they never conceived as possible.'

With that, he took out another cigar and failed to light it in the evening breeze. He lit another match and I put my hands round his to create better protection from the wind. The cigar tip glowed red as he drew on it safely.

What more dramatic way to die as an actor than with a Wellesian shot, perhaps these days by means of a drone-mounted camera tracking over him and hovering above him and his typewriter? His motto could have been 'Have typewriter, will travel' as he restlessly moved from place to place.

Only silence around him waiting for his baritone voice which would not be heard again. Silence all around him, as though in awe at the passing of a great spirit.

But it was a week earlier that he had given that interview which I will never forget. I chanced upon it after I had heard about his passing. These were his tortured words:

You know my first picture would never have been made, never in a million years, if the producer had lived in Hollywood and had any knowledge of Hollywood. It was a total accident, a total piece of luck, like winning $600,000 from a quarter in a jackpot. And it couldn't go on and I knew that. I've always hated Hollywood but I've hated almost everything in the modern world. And Hollywood is the most pleasant place to live in left.

I really shouldn't have stayed in this business because it's too ridiculous. I had a lot of options open, everybody does in life. Everybody who has enough sense to make a movie can make a lot of other things. I should have finished right away because I saw right at the beginning that the odds are against the player here. And are by the nature of movie making. What's wrong with this place is that it's not a market place and the market place is always the enemy of the artist. If they don't like what you do really, I was going to show them that they were wrong and I have spent the rest of my life showing people, trying to prove that what they said was wrong and that's been an enormous waste of spirit and of energy.

I don't believe there is any wisdom in compromise unless you are a politician and, to the extent that movies are not politics, I don't belong in movies. I cannot compromise. When I do something that is compromised it is nothing more than a second-rate director's picture. My pictures don't work at all unless they're done my way. It's not because I think they're better that way. They simply fall apart unless they are done my way.

I am a romantic and I was a romantic in the early nineteenth-century way. I wanted every experience, every kind of thing, so I went to Hollywood in that spirit and I should have left what people said about me being difficult was a lie. I've always wanted to be a white hat and I've always wanted to be remembered as a good guy rather than a difficult genius.

I watched him speaking, mesmerised, as though I was looking at him for the last time.

I was.

He looked pale and desperate, seemingly a man in his last moments – which he was. He was gaunt, if ever Mr Welles could look gaunt, haunted, as if he were finally defeated. The last man in his trench, running out of ammunition and seeing the enemy massing before him. His enemies would never understand him, would never feel sympathy for him. They simply spoke another language and had another agenda, where the profound depths of the human spirit would never be explored and where infantilism in the service of Mammon would always be the final objective. They were not, and have never been, refined members of mankind; they are men of little substance save greed, personal ambition and self-aggrandisement, where crudity and crassness rule unopposed.

But wasn't it always thus?

If you measured the quality versus the quantity of the material produced for mass consumption over the 100 years or so that Hollywood has dominated the entertainment industry, you would walk away disappointed, not inspired. It would be as though dwarfs had ruled an empire which had demanded giants, and Orson Welles was one of those giants left to roam in the desolate regions beyond that city of gold ruled by so many men called Midas. 'I am running out of countries,' he would say.

Welles was cremated, and a stark funeral was hastily arranged by his widow Paola Mori. In a way, that was rather fitting. Welles' long-time teacher, and latterly friend (who'd originally been his mentor), Roger 'Skipper' Hill gave an impromptu eulogy. Although Welles was a larger-than-life personality with a wide circle of acquaintances, only nine people were present at the small Los Angeles gathering.

Mr Welles always seemed to me to have an air of sadness about him. From the magnificent baby son of Beatrice Welles, to the precocious boy with a baby face, to the still baby-faced but handsome man, and then to the gigantically shaped man of later life, he was a Leviathan wrestling with his own demons, like Prometheus eternally chained in his struggle to make profound statements about *la condition humaine.*

'They all said I was a prodigy,' he said to me one morning in Rome, 'but if you look at all the prodigies in history I don't look like any of them!'

Even though he was undeniably fun, funny, loving in many of his relationships, perceptive and quick-witted, melancholy never seemed to be far away. Maybe it's because so much of his work was in black and white, thereby almost dating it and pointing out that it was from a bygone age. Or maybe because he understood human nature more perceptively than most. Passion, deception, dishonesty, betrayal, truth, lies – these were all human traits with which he was familiar and he brought them to the screen in his art.

He once told me that 'being happy' was an overestimated pastime and that you could find joy in many things without being stupidly happy. He thought 'happy' was rather a silly word. 'Content, yes, but not too much. And not for long periods of time. Otherwise you'll become a vegetable. And I don't want to become an Idaho potato.'

'Many people are,' I suggested.

'You are a bit of an elitist, Dorian. Typical of an Englishman of your background. You thought the Irish were potatoes. You English have an air about you. As if you rule the world. But you don't any more, thank God! What the hell would all of us poor outsiders become?' He roared with laughter at his own joke and his eyes twinkled and looked about him as though inviting others to laugh along with him.

'Falstaff didn't think he was superior,' I defended myself.

'Certainly not, I always think Falstaff was a good man. A good man with weaknesses.'

'Like most of us.'

'Maybe you, Dorian, but certainly not me. I am not sure I am good.'

'I think you are,' I said bravely.

Mr Welles bowed, 'Thank you, my boy.'

THE END

Epilogue

There is a monument in Ronda, in Andalusia, Spain, close to where the ashes of Orson Welles rest. On it are written these words. Make of them what you will.

Un hombre no es de donde nace
sino donde elige morir.
Y Ronda fue la elegida, quiso ser un Rondeno mas para siempre.
Sus cenizas fueron depositadas aqui, en el recreo de San Cayetano
Para la eternidad.[*]

---

[*] A man is not from where he is born
But where he chooses to die.
And Ronda was the chosen place where a man from Ronda chose.
His ashes are placed here, in the San Cayetano park
For eternity.